About the Author

Greg Taylor is an expert on the topics discussed in Dan Brown's books, from ancient secret societies and hidden history through to modern research into the mysteries of the mind. For the past ten years Greg has been the editor of the online alternative news portal, "The Daily Grail" (**www.dailygrail.com**), and he is also the editor-in-chief of the Fortean anthology series *Darklore*. Greg has a long history of research into the subjects of alternative history and secret societies. He also has a website devoted to news and articles on Dan Brown's books: The Cryptex (**www.thecryptex.com**)

The Guide to
Dan Brown's
The Lost Symbol

GREG TAYLOR

Daily Grail Publishing

The Guide to Dan Brown's The Lost Symbol
© Greg Taylor 2009.

All rights reserved. No part of this book may be reproduced, stored, or transmitted in any form without permission in writing from the publisher, except by a reviewer who may quote brief passages for review purposes.

This book has not been approved, licensed or endorsed by any entity involved in creating or producing *The Lost Symbol* or *The Da Vinci Code*.

ISBN: 978-0-9807111-2-7

Masonic Cipher and Symbols Font
© 5999 A.L., ODR Lodge #188, F&AM of California
http://www.ODR.org/

House of the Temple image on p. 90 by 'AgnosticPreachersKid', licensed under Creative Commons Attribution ShareAlike 3.0

CONTENTS

Intro. Seeking the Secrets of The Lost Symbol   7

Chapter 1. The Brotherhood of the Rosy Cross   13

Chapter 2. Freemasonry Emerges   25

Chapter 3. The Masonic Foundations of America   45

Chapter 4. Strange Consructions   75

Chapter 5. A Masonic Conspiracy?   115

Chapter 6. The Lost Codes   139

Chapter 7. Mysteries of the Mind   161

Chapter 8. Quest for The Lost Word   177

Appendix 1. The Codes on the Cover   189

Appendix 2. Resources   197

Appendix 3. A View of the Capital   203

Endnotes.   213

INTRODUCTION

SEEKING THE SECRETS OF THE LOST SYMBOL

The secret is how to...write. And Dan Brown surely knows how to do that. When he released his novel *The Da Vinci Code* in 2003, he would have been hoping for some success. In 1996 Dan Brown had taken the biggest gamble of his life, giving up his job as an English teacher at the prestigious Phillips Exeter Academy in order to write fiction novels for a living. His first novel, *Digital Fortress*, explored the controversial debate between national security interests versus civilian privacy, through the medium of one of Brown's favourite hobbies: cryptography. However, despite becoming a #1 national bestselling e-book, *Digital Fortress* only sold moderately well in bookstores.

Two follow-up novels, *Deception Point* and *Angels and Demons*, met with similar receptions, although with the latter Brown hit upon a potent recipe that would carry his next work to great success. In *Angels and Demons* we meet for the first time the now famous character of Robert Langdon, a Harvard Professor of Religious Symbology called in by authorities to help solve mysterious crimes, on account of his comprehensive knowledge of symbols and codes.

Just as *Digital Fortress* juxtaposed national security with civilian privacy, the plot of *Angels and Demons* was based around the dichotomy of science and religion – perhaps a reflection of Brown's own influences, growing up as the son of a Presidential Award-winning math professor and a professional sacred musician. The storyline, which involved an ancient secret society engaged in a centuries-old battle with the Catholic Church, allowed the author to include a number of interesting, though disparate, topics: cutting-edge science, conspiracy theories, religious symbolism and cryptography.

The 'treasure hunt' aspect is a key ingredient in Dan Brown's novels, and is based on his own love of cryptography. During his childhood, his mathematician father would create treasure hunts for his children involving ciphers and codes. Brown would later insert this little bit of personal history into the character of Sophie Neveu in *The Da Vinci Code*. The appeal to the reader is obvious: the cryptographic codes and symbolism draw the reader in on a personal level as they try to solve each problem, while the aspects of 'hidden history' reward through a sense of revelation, the unveiling of secrets. John Chadwick, the philologist and cryptanalyst who helped decipher the early Greek language script 'Linear B', aptly described the human affinity for secrets and puzzles in his book *The Decipherment of Linear B*:

> *The urge to discover secrets is deeply ingrained in human nature; even the least curious mind is roused by the promise of sharing knowledge withheld from others…most of us*

are driven to sublimate this urge by the solving of artificial puzzles devised for our entertainment.[1]

Dan Brown's melding of the detective-thriller genre with the subject of secret societies and alternative histories proved to be an inspirational combination in his next novel *The Da Vinci Code*. Referencing the historical mystery of the secret society known as the Priory of Sion, and embedding legends of art history within his cryptographic puzzles, Brown finally realized his dreams of writing a best-seller – on a massive scale.

Rarely has a novel set such benchmarks. Since its release in 2003, *The Da Vinci Code* has broken sales records all over the globe. As of September 2009, Brown's publisher Random House claims to have sold more than 81 million copies of the book worldwide. As a bonus, the success of the book has meant that his earlier novels are now all best-sellers as well. Amazingly, in early 2004 all four of Brown's novels held places on the *New York Times* bestseller list during the same week – an incredible accomplishment. Not to mention, both *The Da Vinci Code* and *Angels and Demons* have been made into hit films, with Oscar-winners Ron Howard directing and Tom Hanks playing the lead character of Robert Langdon. A movie version of *The Lost Symbol* is already in preproduction, and is scheduled for release in 2012.

The Da Vinci Code has also had a huge sociological influence. Dan Brown's use of heretical themes, such as the marriage of Jesus to Mary Magdalene, has led to widespread controversy and much discussion over the 'true history' of Christianity – and in particular, Catholicism. In March 2005, the Vatican reacted by going on the offensive against Brown's bestseller: in an unprecedented attack on a fictional book, Cardinal Tarcisio Bertone, the Archbishop of Genoa, accused the novel of being "filled with lies and manipulations." Cardinal Bertone described

Dan Brown's heretical plotline as "deplorable", and urged Catholic bookstores to take the thriller off their shelves.

The Lost Symbol Cometh

However, it's worth asking if Dan Brown was just hoping for success, or whether he was in fact planning on it. The initial release of *The Da Vinci Code* was accompanied by the publishing equivalent of a frontal assault. Brown's publisher Doubleday initially sent out some 10,000 free copies of the book to influential reviewers and major bookshops, quite a substantial risk investment as Brown was – at that time – an only moderately successful author. In fact, the number of free copies sent out was around half the number that Brown's previous three novels had sold altogether. The bold move paid off however, with early reviews generating a word-of-mouth campaign which would guarantee profound success for the novel.

Additionally, it is now obvious that Dan Brown was planning very early on for *The Da Vinci Code* to be the first in a series of books that would be marketed together, for on the dust jacket of the U.S. edition of that novel a number of ciphers can be found which reference the subject matter of *The Lost Symbol* – six years in advance! When originally found by readers, the coded messages were ambiguous and confusing to say the least. However, the reason for their inclusion became obvious when Dan Brown announced in an interview that clues about his next novel could be found on the dust jacket of *The Da Vinci Code*. Soon after, Brown's official website announced a competition titled "Uncover the Code: The Secret is Hidden Right Before Your Eyes."

The inclusion of the codes on the book jacket was a masterstroke on the part of Brown and his publisher, and one which showed admirable foresight. Hundreds of thousands of fans participated in the competition on Brown's website, and Internet forums were deluged with long threads discussing the solutions. Then, in the lead-up to the release of *The Lost Symbol*, Dan Brown and his publisher released more hints about the content via Facebook and Twitter.[2] Building on the air of expectation by slowly revealing hints about the next book, Brown managed to generate an almost hysterical level of anticipation for the long-awaited sequel to *The Da Vinci Code*.

Seeking Answers

Now that the book is out, readers finally know the plot and characters of *The Lost Symbol*. But how well do they know the topics? Freemasonry is a secret society – or as members would rather it, a "society with secrets"– that most readers have very little knowledge of. Brown quickly touches on a number of fascinating topics to do with Freemasonry – from its links with the beginning the modern scientific era, to its impact on the Founding Fathers of the United States – without exploring them in detail. But *The Lost Symbol* casts its nets far wider than just Freemasonry. Dan Brown casually mentions a number of aspects of the 'hidden history' of the United States, such as the role played by another secret society, the "Rosicrucians", in the founding of the nation. Important historical figures such as Sir Francis Bacon are briefly referred to, without much discussion of how they fit into the story. The Deist and Utopian ideals of the Founding Fathers are also referenced, and then suddenly dropped. And the esoteric secrets and cutting-edge science that Dan Brown discusses in the book certainly deserve a little more scrutiny, given their importance to humanity if they contain even a grain of truth.

Perhaps Dan Brown wanted to leave it to the reader to seek out more information about these enigmatic topics. If so, then this guide is exactly what you are looking for. In each chapter we'll explore the 'big' concepts' in *The Lost Symbol*: the origins of Freemasonry, the secrets of the Ancient Mysteries, and the cutting-edge Noetic Science which may well change our worldview. If you're looking for trivia and fact-checking of the minutiae, this isn't the book for you. By reading this guide, I hope that you'll learn more about these fascinating ideas and have a better understanding of the major topics when the inevitable debates over *The Lost Symbol* begin. Let's get started...

CHAPTER 1

THE BROTHERHOOD OF THE ROSY CROSS

In the two previous Robert Langdon novels Dan Brown used secret societies as a major theme of each book. In *Angels and Demons* it was the Illuminati, while in *The Da Vinci Code* it was the Priory of Sion. Now, in *The Lost Symbol,* Dan Brown has turned his eyes towards Freemasonry. While there are considerable doubts about the pedigree of the Priory of Sion, both the Illuminati and Freemasonry were very real historical groups (though, it must be said, Dan Brown's version of the Illuminati was largely fictional in its details). Freemasonry has definitely survived into modern times, while the 'Bavarian Illuminati' appears to have survived for less than a decade in the 18th century – although numerous conspiracy theorists would say they just went 'underground' after this point and not only survive to this day, but are also a major influence behind world events.

In response to a query regarding his fascination with secret societies, Brown answered with these words:

> *My interest sparks from growing up in New England, surrounded by the clandestine clubs of Ivy League universities, the Masonic lodges of our Founding Fathers, and the hidden hallways of early government power...*[3]

A mass of contradictory literature is available on Masonry, and it's often difficult to figure out where the legends end and truth begins when it comes to the history of this enigmatic group. Superficially thought of by those not completely familiar with it either as a quaint but innocent 'old boys' network, or alternately as a Machiavellian organization of subversive power, in the following pages we'll have a look at the origins of the society, and how it has impacted upon American history in a significant way.

Both the Illuminati and Masons are part of a tradition which is often referred to as 'Rosicrucian'. The Rosicrucian groups encompassed numerous beliefs and political allegiances, but can perhaps be best tied together by the similarity of their aspirations. In *The Lost Symbol*, Dan Brown often makes reference to this tradition – and some of the key individuals involved, such as Sir Francis Bacon – without expanding on its significance to the storyline, and most especially, to the history of the United States. To understand the beginnings of these groups, we need to travel back in time some five hundred years, and explore the political and religious climate of Europe at the time, as well as the emergence of modern science from the 'Enlightenment' period. This quick diversion through history will prove enormously helpful in understanding the importance of Rosicrucian thinking to Freemasonry and the possible motivations of the Founding Fathers of the United States.

A Divided Europe

The start of the 16th century saw the beginnings of massive turmoil in Europe. The Catholic Church had become morally and financially corrupt. Monarchies throughout Europe had begun asserting their rule in Draconian style, removing constitutional restrictions on their authority. Additionally, as a result of the stress of the rapid changes occurring in societies across the continent, trouble began to ferment just beneath the surface of daily life. It could be argued that a lightning bolt quite literally ignited the impending inferno...

In 1505 a young German man was returning from school when lightning struck the ground near him. Terrified, he immediately made a promise in return for salvation: "Help, St. Anne! I'll become a monk." Soon realizing that he had survived, the 21-year-old Martin Luther kept his word, and dropped out of law school and entered a monastery. However, despite a fervent love for Christianity, it did not take long for the young man to become disillusioned with the Church.

Luther's dislike of the endemic greed and corruption within the Catholic Church boiled over in 1517, when he delivered a sermon attacking the practice of selling indulgences. As part of his attack, he also nailed a document to the door of the castle church for debate. Luther's document condemned the Church's greed and secularism. The young Catholic obviously touched a nerve in European society – within two weeks Luther's manifesto had spread throughout Germany, and soon after it was being read and discussed across Europe. The Reformation had begun, and Europe was about to be split into two religious camps – Catholic and Protestant.

In England the Reformation heralded a new era, with Henry VIII finding it politically expedient to break with Rome. Large amounts of Catholic property were taken over by the monarchy, and much of it passed into the hands of the nobility. With such rewards for those supporting the Reformation, the result was obvious. It is in this 'new' England that we find some of the key characters emerging in the beginnings of Rosicrucianism.

THE LAST MAGICIAN

In parallel with the religious revolution of the Reformation came another challenge to Church authority. Towards the end of the 15th century a small group in Florence had ushered in the era of Western esotericism. Centered on the Renaissance philosopher Marsilio Ficino, the catalyst for this ground-breaking moment was the translation of various ancient texts, including those from Christian mysticism, Neoplatonism, Gnosticism, and the Corpus Hermeticum. Translated into Latin in 1471, the Corpus Hermeticum in particular had a huge impact on the intellectual milieu of the time, with its alleged authorship by the legendary Hermes Trismegistus. Ficino's work inspired another young Florentine, Giovanni Pico della Mirandola, to integrate the Jewish mystical tradition of Kabbalah into this esoteric mix. Then, at the start of the 16th century, much of this occult wisdom was collected and elaborated on in perhaps the most influential book on magic and the occult in human history: *De occulta philosophia* ('The Occult Philosophy'), by Heinrich Cornelius Agrippa. In the words of esoteric scholar Henrik Bogdan, in this seminal work "the natural magic of Ficino and the Kabbalah of Pico are combined with the art of alchemy, and thus the three 'jewels' of Western esotericism: magic, astrology, and alchemy are linked together."[4] The esoteric revival spread across Europe quickly in subsquent years, and in England was welcomed by a remarkable individual.

The legendary Elizabethan philosopher John Dee (1527–1609) was the very definition of a 'Renaissance Man'. A respected mathematician, astronomer and geographer, he was also astrologer to Queen Elizabeth and a serious student of alchemy, Kabbalah, and magick. His knowledge of navigation meant that he taught many of the great explorers of the time, and he had the ear of the Queen of England, who held him in high regard.

Despite being a pious Christian, Dee was also fascinated by occultism. The Hermetic and Kabbalistic philosophies of Pico della Mirandola were a great influence, as was Agrippa's division of the universe into natural, celestial, and supercelestial worlds.[5] To many today he is remembered mostly for his attempted communication with the celestial hierarchies of the angels, a practice still undertaken by modern occultists under the title 'Enochian Magic'. While his activities might seem to us today as heretical, and contradictory to his Christian belief, the religious landscape was of a different kind at that time. The respected scholar Dame Frances Yates points out that during the Renaissance, Hermetic and Kabbalistic studies were not discouraged by the Catholic Church, and in fact cardinals were known to dabble in some of these areas. The status of magick however was far more tentative, with the ever-present danger of being labeled as being in league with the Devil.

Dee though would have felt that his magick was of a Christian leaning, as he was attempting to contact the angels, not summoning demons. Indeed, his ultimate goal was to help unify Europe by uncovering the pure religion of the ancients, thus healing any denominational schisms. Yates finds in Dee the beginnings of what she termed the 'Rosicrucian Enlightenment':[6] with Protestantism allowing more latitude in the tolerance of occult practices, the beginnings of science were nurtured as these 'magicians' experimented in alchemy and natural philosophy. However, Yates says that the occult-leaning Dee was expunged from history as the inspiration for both modern science and Rosicrucianism by those fearing the repercussions of the later witch-hunts.

In *The Rosicrucian Enlightenment,* Frances Yates describes Dee as a "towering figure" who was the major influence behind the original Rosicrucian movement. And the key to this movement was the philosophy of *inclusion,* the idea that humanity could only move forward by being tolerant of all religious attitudes – one of the key themes of *The Lost Symbol.*

The Advancement of Learning

The dawn of the 17th century was an amazing period of discovery. The heretical idea of Copernicus – that the Earth actually revolved around the Sun – began getting serious attention. The figures of Galileo and Kepler impose their monumental influence upon history. And an English gentleman by the name of Francis Bacon unofficially inaugurated one of the world's greatest scientific institutions.

Sir Francis Bacon (1561-1626) was the youngest of five sons born to Sir Nicholas Bacon, the 'Keeper of the Great Seal' to Queen Elizabeth I. As a man of extraordinary intelligence, Bacon had become dissatisfied with the methods and results of the 'sciences' of the time. Thus he took it upon himself to institute a new mode of learning, in parallel with his influential political and legal career during the reigns of both Elizabeth I and James I. In his 1605 publication *The Advancement of Learning,* Bacon pronounced much of the present state of knowledge to be deficient. He argued for a brotherhood of learning, whereby learned men could exchange ideas independent of their beliefs and political allegiances. Here we find a curious echo of Dee's desire for inclusion, a pan-sophism where knowledge belongs to all men.

In his *Novus Organum* ('New Organ'), Bacon put forth his own ideas on how the quest for knowledge could be refined.

Intended as a replacement for the great philosopher Aristotle's original *Organum*, this book established a far more rigorous scientific procedure, which has become known as the Baconian method. This method of investigation takes note of many possible experimental fallacies, such as the human tendency to see patterns in random systems, incorrect method, and personal bias. It would become one of the cornerstones of the impending scientific revolution that would catapult the world forward into a new age of discovery and technological advance.

Bacon continued to publish his thoughts on the advancement of knowledge until his bizarre death in 1626. Inspired by the possibility of using snow to preserve meat, Bacon had purchased a chicken from the market and set out to evaluate the hypothesis himself, in true scientific style. However, the process of stuffing the chicken with snow was too much for his fragile health, and he contracted a fatal case of pneumonia from the cold and died soon after. However, subsequent to his death, one more extremely influential essay was published, *The New Atlantis,* which we will discuss soon.

Sir Francis Bacon

The Rosicrucians Arrive

During Bacon's lifetime a number of strange texts suddenly appeared, which despite their obscurity soon began to have a dramatic influence throughout Europe. In 1614 and 1615, in the German town of Kassel, two mysterious manuscripts were published with no hint as to who had authored them. Their curious titles were the *Frama Fraternitatis* ("*The Fame of the Praiseworthy Order of the Rosy Cross*") and the *Confessio Fraternitatis* ("*Confession of the Fraternity*").

These manuscripts told the mythical story of a German man named Christian Rosenkreutz, who was born in 1378 and traveled to the Holy Land and the Middle East at age 16. While there, he came across a Utopian-like community, which was governed only by "wise and understanding men". Rosenkreutz was also initiated into occult mysteries and the ancient 'secret wisdom' while on his pilgrimage.

The texts also say that once back in Germany, Rosenkreutz formed the 'Fraternity of the Rosy Cross' in 1407 with a number of like-minded individuals. The group made it their mission to travel the world, spreading the ancient teachings and healing the sick.

Rosenkreutz was said to have died in 1484, at the ripe old age of 106. As the story goes, a small group of initiates continued on with their founder's important work, until in 1604 one of the brethren uncovered a hidden door leading to the tomb of their master. Upon opening a door inscribed with the prophecy "after 120 years I shall open", they found a seven-sided vault filled with symbols, books and other wondrous objects. One of the treasures was the so-called 'Book M', reputed to have been written by King Solomon himself, and in which he recorded "all things past, present, and to come". Standing in the middle of the crypt was a coffin containing the perfectly preserved body of

Christian Rosenkreutz. This was taken as a sign that the general public should be made aware of the existence of the Order, and that invitations should be issued for like-minded people to join them in their quest.[7]

The revelation that this secret society was coming forth caused immense excitement across Europe. The changes happening throughout society at that time meant that a lot of people could identify with the Rosicrucian message: the spreading of a reconstituted ancient wisdom, guiding the population towards a new Utopia. Famous scientists and philosophers began attempting to track down or contact the Rosicrucian fraternity, in order to join, although with no luck. The feeling was that Europe was entering a new age of enlightenment, guided by the 'truth' of the ancients, leading them back to the "Paradisal state before the Fall."[8]

Who were these anonymous brethren committed to reshaping the world? Detailed research has failed to uncover any real members of the original Rosicrucian society, and all evidence points to the documents (as well as the subsequent release *The Chymical Wedding of Christian Rosenkreutz*) being the fictitious creation of a German theologian named Johann Valentin Andreae. No fraternity ever existed – and Andreae actually made extensive efforts during his lifetime to correct the misunderstanding that the Rosicrucian Manifestos were literal documents.

Nevertheless, the myth had engendered a reality. Though fiction, they provided a model for what was needed in the material world. A major part of the Utopia prophesized by the Rosicrucians was the recommendation that learned men of different backgrounds collaborate for the good of all mankind. Strangely enough, this is exactly what happened soon after in England.

The Invisible College

At the time of his death, Sir Francis Bacon had been working on a Utopian myth of his own, *The New Atlantis*. Though incomplete, it was nevertheless published in 1627, one year after his passing and just over a decade after the release of the Rosicrucian documents in Germany. In *The New Atlantis*, Bacon set out his dream of a perfect society where religion and science co-exist in harmony. It tells the story of navigators who discover a new land, in which they find this perfect society. Within this culture, there is a group of priest-scientists organized in a college called Solomon's House, which is dedicated to the quest for illuminating knowledge and the advancement of humanity. The necessary link back to ancient wisdom is made here, with Bacon also saying that the New Atlantis has possession of some of the lost works of King Solomon.

The curious thing about *The New Atlantis* is that, despite there being no explicit references to the Fraternity of the Rosy Cross in its pages, it is quite obvious that it is a Rosicrucian document. Frances Yates has raised solid evidence to prove this point, not least that one of the officials of the Utopian Atlantis wears a white turban "with a small red cross on the top."[9] Indeed, Solomon's House sounds extremely similar to the Rosicrucian fraternity.

Yates points out that another author by the name of John Heydon recorded his recognition of this similarity three decades later in his *Holy Guide*. This book was basically an adaptation of *The New Atlantis*, except in Heydon's version the 'House of Solomon' is replaced by "the wise Men of the Society of the Rosicrucians."[10] And he expands Bacon's 'lost works of Solomon' to include the legendary 'Book M' found in the tomb of Christian Rosenkreutz.

The obvious question to be raised is this: was *The New Atlantis* inspired by the Rosicrucian manifestos, or were the manifestos originally written in response to Bacon's earlier work and as such appeared to presage Bacon's Utopian allegory? A third possibility also emerges, one that we will explore further in the next chapter: that both Bacon and Andreae were influenced by an earlier tradition.

The publication of Sir Francis Bacon's *The New Atlantis*, in combination with the Rosicrucian Manifestos, led to an almost feverish expectancy that a great change was afoot. Utopians gathered in England, the home of Bacon. The Utopian Samuel Hartlib wrote his own fiction, *A Description of the Famous Kingdom of Macaria*, and addressed it to the English Parliament, confidently predicting that they would "lay the corner stone of the worlds happinesse." The great educator, Comenius, professed his wish that agents of change begin spreading throughout the known world, and intriguingly added that these people must be guided by an order...

> ...*so that each of them may know what he has to do, and for whom and when and with what assistance, and may set about his business in a manner which will make for the public benefit.*[11]

However, the Utopian dream was to be put on hold when England descended into civil war in 1642, leading to the abolition of the monarchy and the beginnings of the protectorate of Oliver Cromwell. Or at least the public face of the Utopians disappeared, as around this time we see the first records emerging of an 'Invisible College'. Pioneering Scottish chemist Robert Boyle, who went on to develop the eponymous Boyle's Law (that the volume of a gas varies inversely with the pressure), mentions this society in a letter dated February 1647:

> *The best on't is, that the cornerstones of the Invisible or (as they term themselves) the Philosophical College, do*

> *now and then honour me with their company...men of so capacious and searching spirits...persons that endeavour to put narrow-mindedness out of countenance, by the practice of so extensive a charity that it reaches unto everything called man, and nothing less than an universal good-will can content it...they take the whole body of mankind to their care.*

The Invisible College is believed to be the antecedent to the more famous scientific institution, the Royal Society, which has boasted some of the greatest minds of the past few centuries (Sir Isaac Newton being one of many). Inaugurated in 1660, at the time of the restoration of the throne to England, the Society included a number of both parliamentarians and monarchists, brought together in the quest for knowledge. Frances Yates notes that at this point, the goals of the organization appear to have changed, at least outwardly:

> *...the situation was tricky. There were many subjects which had to be avoided: utopian schemes for reform belonged to the revolutionary past which it was now better to forget... witch-scares were not altogether a thing of the past.*[12]

The Royal Society is now viewed by many as the inspiration for modern science. To be sure, a number of members were rationalists, following in the mode of Francis Bacon. But also present were alchemists, Hermeticists and Kabbalists – Newton himself was an alchemist who did not believe in the Catholic doctrine of the Holy Trinity. And lurking beneath the surface of the Royal Society was another secret society, one which returns us to the central topic of *The Lost Symbol*: Freemasonry.

CHAPTER 2

FREEMASONRY EMERGES

Now that we have a basic understanding of the background to the Rosicrucian movement, we should be better able to understand the origins of Freemasonry. Freemasonry is often described as "a peculiar system of morality veiled in allegory and illustrated by symbols." It is a secret society, complete with coded words and secret handshakes, which uses a graded system of initiation – thus maintaining a hierarchical system of members who are exposed to 'deeper mysteries' as they move further up the ladder. The 'system of morality' uses as its metaphor the theme of the stone mason, using raw materials and certain tools to construct a polished temple, in conjunction with legends originating in the Judaic tradition.

These legends tell of the building of Solomon's Temple, an event mentioned in Judaic commentaries, the Christian Old Testament, as well as in Islamic sources. After succeeding his father David, Solomon decided to build a great temple, and enlisted the help of the king of the neighboring country of Tyre:

> *Thou knowest how that David my father could not build an house unto the name of the Lord his God for the wars which were about him on every side, until the Lord put them under the soles of his feet. But now the Lord my God hath given me rest on every side, so that there is neither adversary nor evil occurrent. And, behold, I purpose to build an house unto the name of the Lord my God...*[13]

In the Old Testament commentary, we find present two elements which would become important parts of Masonic iconography – the twin pillars named Jachin and Boaz (which turn up in *The Lost Symbol* in the form of tattoos on Mal'akh's legs), and the designation of an architect/builder named Hiram as "the widow's son":

> *King Solomon sent for Hiram of Tyre; he was the son of a widow of the tribe of Naphtali but his father had been a Tyrian, a bronzeworker. He came to King Solomon and did all this work for him: He cast two bronze pillars... and he set up the right pillar, and called the name thereof Jachin: and he set up the left pillar, and called the name thereof Boaz.*[14]

The legends of Masonry tell more about this Hiram than is mentioned in the Bible commentary. Naming him as 'Hiram Abiff', the Craft mythology sees him as a master architect, skilled in geometry and mathematics. Hiram, as the Master Mason, presided over three grades of workers on the Temple – apprentices, fellows and masters – with particular handshakes and secret words being used to designate each level of Mason.

Masonic legend tells that near the completion of Solomon's Temple, Hiram was praying alone when he was confronted by three 'fellows' seeking the 'Master's word'. When Hiram refused to pass on this secret information, he was then assaulted by the trio. The legend tells that each of the villains inflicted a particular wound upon Hiram at three of the cardinal points of the Temple (north, south and west): he is hit on the head by a hammer, as well as on each temple by a plumb and a level. Hiram staggers to the exit on the eastern side of the Temple, but collapses and dies.

The murderers proceed to hide the body of Hiram, burying it beneath a sprig of acacia. It is not until seven days later that the corpse is found, at which point it is exhumed and reinterred with proper ceremony. At the funeral, the Master Masons all wear white gloves and aprons, a symbolic gesture to show that they are not stained with the murdered man's blood.

While it is difficult for us to attach a deeper meaning to this legend, there is little doubt that it is a 'blind' which disguises some secret. Perhaps it is an allegory referring to nature religions, or maybe it is a coded reference to the archaic ritual killings sometimes used to consecrate a new building in the ancient world. Whatever its meaning, the legend and many of the symbols that go with it (such as the acacia, the apron, the cardinal directions in the Temple) are of profound importance to the core of Freemasonry.

As an aside, it is interesting to note that Michael Baigent and Richard Leigh, in their book *The Temple and the Lodge*, raise the possibility that Solomon built his temple in honor of the Phoenician mother goddess Astarte – the 'Queen of Heaven'.[15] They cite evidence from the Old Testament, which explicitly says that Solomon became a follower of Astarte. It is also said that the well-known 'Song of Solomon' is in fact a hymn to Astarte. In terms of Dan Brown's use of the 'sacred feminine' theme in *The Da Vinci Code*, it's almost a shame to see that this fact was not mentioned in *The Lost Symbol*.

Modern Freemasonry has become somewhat of an enigma. Described by some as the secret power behind world governments, it is conversely thought by others to simply be an archaic 'old boys club' performing rituals of which members have no understanding. It claims a pedigree going back to ancient Egypt and the Temple of Solomon, and yet historical evidence suggests it is a (relatively) modern invention. It espouses an egalitarian doctrine free from prejudice, and yet it maintains its secrecy, uses an internal hierarchy, and is restricted to male applicants. These contradictory attributes of Freemasonry, though perhaps overstated, are often the main sources of criticism of the 'Craft'.

The Official History

The official history of Freemasonry begins with the inauguration of the Grand Lodge in London on June 24th, 1717 – though this was certainly not the 'start' of Freemasonry. The Grand Lodge acted as a governing body for a number of individual lodges which already existed at this time, establishing standard practices to which other lodges were directed to conform. How far back these individual lodges go is somewhat of an ambiguous question: there had been lodges of 'Operative Masons' (professional stonemasons) for centuries, but during the 17th century we start seeing 'non-operatives' as members of lodges, and the beginnings of 'Speculative Masonry' – the modern Freemasonry we know today.

Early documents referring to Operative Masonry – known as the Old Charges – include the Regius Manuscript (1390) and the Cooke Manuscript (1425). These offer some of the first recorded instances of the Masonic mythos claiming an ancestry back to ancient Egypt and Greece – although in the words of one historian, they may be dismissed as "impressive exercises in the dubious skills of name-dropping and creative chronology."[16] It is not until the mid-1600s that we see lodges in Scotland beginning to admit non-stonemasons – but what caused this change? One theory is that the lodges became more of a 'club', and so non-mason acquaintances began to be invited to join. Over time the number of non-operatives grew, until they became the majority and Speculative Masonry began to evolve in the place of practical masonic discussion.

Jay Kinney presents another theory worth considering, in his excellent book *The Masonic Myth*:

> *Historian David Stevenson has suggested that after William Schaw was appointed Master of the Works by King James VI of Scotland in 1583, Schaw reorganized the Scottish lodge system in a more orderly fashion – including the taking of minutes – and introduced some elements of Renaissance esotericism into Masonic practice. The formal rules for this reorganized Masonry, known as the first and second Schaw Statutes, include an order that entered apprentices and fellow crafts be tested in "the art of memory and science thairof." Stevenson suggests that this may well refer to "the Art of Memory" – a practice championed by such Renaissance esotericists as Giordano Bruno... Stevenson thus credits Schaw with hatching a deeper, more speculative Freemasonry within Scottish Masonry itself.*

Initially, there were two levels of initiation in Masonry: the 'Entered Apprentice', which was followed by 'Fellow Craft'. Soon after a third 'degree' was added, that of the 'Master Mason' (the intense questioning of the candidate which occurs during the initiation ceremony now gives its name to any intense interrogation: to be 'given the third degree'). These three standard degrees are commonly referred to as 'blue' Freemasonry, and are based on the legend of Hiram as mentioned earlier.

The official movement soon spread into Europe, with the French educated classes showing a particular affinity for the fraternal society. The first Grand Lodge of France was founded in Paris at some point during the 1730s. Once in France, the Craft began to evolve somewhat, with the addition of chivalric themes and mystical elements to the Mason mythos. Out of this development came various new species of Freemasonry, including the 'Scottish Rite', which claimed a heritage back to the Knights Templar.

You may be curious as to why a French system of Masonry became known as Scottish Rite. This is due largely to the influence of a Scottish émigré named Andrew Michael Ramsay, who claimed in an introductory speech written for initiates – referred to as the 'Oration' – that Masonry arose out of the Crusades and the Knights Templar organization, and that this authentic tradition was preserved by Scottish Masonry. New rites and degrees were added to the basic Craft initiation, based on a mystical story relating back to the building of Solomon's Temple. For example, in the Scottish Rite, Freemasons can seek initiation into further degrees, numbered 4 to 32 (with the final degree, the 33rd, being an honorary degree bestowed upon the 'worthy'). These added degrees beyond the first three are often referred to as 'red' Masonry.

Other species of Masonry continued to be spawned as the Craft spread across Europe, into Germany, Prussia and elsewhere. German Masonry was dominated for a time by the 'Strict Observance', founded in 1760, and which once again emphasized a Templar tradition behind the brotherhood. Later modifications included the 'York Rite' and 'Rectified Scottish Rite', and some lodges started to incorporate Egyptian influences as well. Even the Grand Lodge of England was challenged by the 'Grand Lodge of the Antients', formed in 1751 in reaction to modifications in Masonic rituals and other traditions. English (and to an extent, American) Masonic lodges remained divided between the 'Moderns' and the 'Antients' until 1813, when the two Grand Lodges put their differences aside and formed the United Grand Lodge of England (often referred to as as UGLE).

A secret society that failed to observe strict Christian doctrine was bound to arouse the suspicion of the Church, based on the possibility of a conspiracy to undermine their authority. Sure enough, Pope Clement XII condemned Freemasonry in 1738, as did Pope Benedict XIV in 1751. While these papal orders were often not implemented by local authorities, suspicions about the Craft continued, with Lodges barely being tolerated in many regions. However, despite continued negative publicity throughout its history, today there are more than 10,000 Masonic lodges covering practically every corner of the globe. In the United States there are around 1.5 million Freemasons, a third of whom are also involved in the Scottish Rite. And given the positive light that Dan Brown has shone upon the Brotherhood in *The Lost Symbol*, you would have to imagine those numbers will now rise dramatically.

Masonry's Speculative History

When Andrew Ramsay enunciated the connection between the Craft and the Knights Templar, it was certainly not fashionable to do so. This group of crusading knights – under the official name of the 'Poor Knights of Christ and the Temple of Solomon' – had been disbanded in the early 14th century under accusations of debauchery and sacrilege.

On Friday the 13th, 1307, King Philippe IV of France had ordered the arrest of all Templars in his domains. The operation was done under an amazing veil of secrecy, with sealed orders being opened by the King's men only shortly before the action to minimize the Templars' foreknowledge of the impending catastrophe. The Catholic 'Inquisition' then took over where Philippe left off, and Templars throughout Europe were interrogated, imprisoned, and often executed with bizarre accusations being leveled against them. The Pope dissolved the Templar order in 1312, and in 1314 Jacques de Molay, the last Grand-Master of the Knights Templar, was burned at the stake.[17]

Under intense interrogations Templar knights admitted to strange behaviour, and rumors began to circulate about the true nature of this supposedly 'holy' Order. Charges against them included spitting and trampling on the cross, of obscene kisses during initiations, and that they worshipped a devil called 'Baphomet'. After so many centuries, it is difficult now to really know which charges may have had some substance. As Baigent, Leigh and Lincoln point out in *Holy Blood, Holy Grail*, trying to do so by studying the records of the Inquisition is a little like trying to get the facts about the activities of the French resistance during World War II by studying the records of the Gestapo.[18]

Nevertheless, certain accusations seem to have had some basis. For example, the worship of 'Baphomet' turns up regularly, too many times to be a coincidence. Dan Brown mentions it in *The Da Vinci Code*, describing Baphomet as a "pagan fertility god associated with the creative force of reproduction." According to him, the Templars honored Baphomet by encircling a stone replica of his horned head whilst chanting prayers. Brown also has his characters decrypt the word 'Baphomet' via the Atbash Cipher, which translates it into 'Sophia', the Greek word for 'wisdom'.

Despite the apparent ingenuity of Robert Langdon and company, this decryption was actually first publicized by Dr

Hugh Schonfield in *The Essene Odyssey*. In his book, published in 1985, Schonfield discusses the Jewish rebel sect known as the Essenes, who are thought by some to have constructed the Dead Sea settlement and also authored the now-famous ancient scrolls found there. The Essenes employed codes in some of their writings, one of which is the Atbash Cipher. The cipher is a straight substitution between two Hebrew alphabets, one written forward and the other in reverse (first for last, second for second-last etc). Hugh Schonfield applied the Atbash to what he believed was the "artificial name Baphomet", and was surprised to find it revealed the name of the Goddess of Wisdom. The implication of Schonfield's discovery is that the Templars may have been the protectors of Essene secrets, and may also have had a reverence for the mystery religions of the ancient goddesses.

This possibility of a Templar fascination with the 'sacred feminine' may be backed up by Andrew Ramsay's 'Oration', mentioned above, given in 1737 and linking Masonry and the Templars. For in it he says:

> Yes, sirs, the famous festivals of Ceres at Eleusis, of Isis in Egypt, of Minerva at Athens, of Urania amongst the Phenicians, and of Diana in Scythia were connected with ours. In those places mysteries were celebrated which concealed many vestiges of the ancient religion of Noah and the Patriarchs.[19]

While the revelation that the Scottish Rite identifies itself with the ancient mystery schools of the sacred goddesses is certainly a pleasant surprise, given Freemasonry's 'male-only' membership requirement, it is also pertinent to note that Ramsay does not condone any 'Hieros Gamos'-like practices – indeed he gives such corruptions as a reason for the exclusion of females from the Craft:

> *The source of these infamies was the admission to the nocturnal assemblies of persons of both sexes in contravention of the primitive usages. It is in order to prevent similar abuses that women are excluded from our Order. We are not so unjust as to regard the fair sex as incapable of keeping a secret. But their presence might insensibly corrupt the purity of our maxims and manners.*[20]

Schonfield's discovery of the Atbash cipher also creates a link between two organizations more than a millennium apart. So what Essene secrets might the Templars have been privy to? In *The Hiram Key*, Chris Knight and Robert Lomas argue that ideas found in the Dead Sea Scrolls are very similar to Freemasonry, and this proves a continuity of tradition from Essene to Freemason through the Templars.

Interestingly, one of the Dead Sea Scrolls, known as the 'Copper Scroll', makes reference to twenty four separate hoards of treasure reputedly secreted away beneath the Temple.[21] This cache is said to be comprised of treasure of all types – bullion, sacred objects, and a number of scrolls as well. And the Knights Templar, while crusading in the Holy Land, were known to have stationed themselves in the vicinity of the Temple Mount. Were they there to search for the treasure?

It is certainly possible. In the book *Digging Up Jerusalem*, authored by respected archaeologist Kathleen Kenyon, we are told that a group of the British Army Royal Engineers surveyed and excavated the Temple Mount in the late 19th century.[22] And, according to the testimony of Robert Brydon, the Templar archivist for Scotland, this British Army contingent unearthed already existing tunnels in which were found a part of a Templar sword, the remains of a lance, and a Templar cross. No treasure was found. Did the Templars find it first? Modern scholars dispute the claim – but such trivialities don't bother Dan Brown.

In *The Da Vinci Code*, Brown assumes the Templars found something and writes his novel accordingly. In his words, "four chests of documents" were found under the site of Solomon's Temple, "documents that have been the object of countless Grail quests throughout history" – perhaps including a text written by Jesus himself and the 'diary' of Mary Magdalene recording her personal relationship with Jesus. These are Brown's 'Sangreal' documents, which form part of the Holy Grail along with the body of Mary Magdalene.

In *The Second Messiah*, Knight and Lomas go on to provide an alternative history of the naming of America, which involves the Essenes, Knights Templar and Freemasons:

> *Josephus records that the Essenes (and therefore the Jerusalem Church) believed that good souls reside beyond the ocean to the west, in a region that is not oppressed with storms of rain, snow or intense heat, but has refreshing gentle breezes.*
>
> *This was also the description given by a people called the Mandaeans who have lived in Southern Iraq since they left Jerusalem shortly after the crucifixion of Jesus, in order to escape the purges of Paul. These Jews left Jerusalem in the first century AD and, according to their traditional history, John the Baptist was the first leader of the Nasoreans and Jesus was a subsequent leader who betrayed special secrets that had been entrusted to him. The Mandaeans still conduct baptism in the river, have special handshakes and practise rituals said to resemble those of Freemasonry. For them this wonderful land across the sea has only the purest spirits, so perfect that mortal eyes cannot see them. This wonderful place is marked by a star called Merica, that sits in the sky above it.*

> We believe that this star and the mythical land below it were known to the Knights Templar from the scrolls that they discovered, and that they sailed in search of 'La Merica' or, as we now know it, America, immediately after their Order had been outlawed.

Dan Brown has gone on record as saying that *The Da Vinci Code* was partly influenced by the books of Knight and Lomas, so it's surprising that he didn't take advantage of this particular 'hidden history' theory in a book dealing with both the secret history of the United States, and Freemasonry.

In *Holy Blood, Holy Grail* the Essenes are described as a mystically oriented Jewish sect, with both Greek and Egyptian influences. Like the Rosicrucian tradition, they were interested in healing, and esoteric studies such as astrology and the Kabbalah. The members of this reclusive religious community were also said to have been keen followers of the teachings of Pythagoras, with a substantial devotion to numerology.[23]

Returning to the Knights Templar: beyond the Atbash Cipher, there also seems to be evidence that the Templars dabbled in alchemy, mysticism and the Kabbalah, much like the Essenes. Interestingly, especially in terms of our investigation, they may also have held as an ideal the possibility of uniting all religions and nations. In light of these attributes, it would seem that the Templars were very much in the Rosicrucian tradition. The fact that the Templars wore as their insignia a red cross might be evidence that the author of the Rosicrucian tracts was attempting to directly link the fraternity to the Knights of Solomon's Temple. Especially so when we consider that Sir Francis Bacon portrayed his priests of the 'House of Solomon' wearing a red cross on their turban.

With Dan Brown's mention of Pythagoras in *The Lost Symbol* (in connection with the veneration of the number 33), we can now see how this 'secret tradition' preserving the Ancient Mysteries likely unfolds in the mythos of Dan Brown's fictional world: Pythagoras to Essenes, Essenes to Knights Templar, Knights Templar to Rosicrucians, Rosicrucians to Freemasons. However, how do we explain the three centuries between the suppression of the Knights Templar and the appearance of the Rosicrucian manifestos?

The Templars Live

Despite the great secrecy surrounding Philippe's action against the Order, it would seem that the Templars – to some extent at least – knew what was coming. Jacques de Molay allegedly called in many of the Order's documents shortly before the arrests and had them burnt. A young knight who withdrew from the Order at this time was told he was extremely wise to do so, as a catastrophe was coming.[24]

In *Holy Blood, Holy Grail* the authors claim that a certain group of knights – all connected to the organization's treasurer – disappeared before the 'October surprise', taking with them the remaining documents and treasure of the Temple. According to one rumor, they boarded a fleet of eighteen ships at La Rochelle and were never heard of again.

Michael Baigent and Richard Leigh pick up the trail of these missing knights in their book about Freemasonry, *The Temple and the Lodge*. They assert that these knights may well have fled to Scotland, taking sides with Robert the Bruce in his fight against England. They were not the first to arrive at such a conclusion, with Templar historians of the 19th century coming to much the same conclusion:

> *The Templars...perhaps found a refuge in the little army of the excommunicated King Robert, whose fear*

of offending the French monarch would doubtless be vanquished by his desire to secure a few capable men-at-arms as recruits.[25]

The Masonic rite of the Strict Observance, created by Baron Karl von Hund in the late 18th century, also claims that the Templars escaped to Scotland – though modern Masonic and Templar historians dispute such theories. For instance, Robert Cooper states that these 'histories' were in reality constructions of the various branches of Freemasonry in order to make sense of their rituals and symbols, and more importantly, "they were invented for allegorical purposes...they were not intended to be taken as literally true."

In any case, Baigent and Leigh – whose writings were so influential on the storyline of *The Da Vinci Code* that they launched a plagiarism lawsuit against Dan Brown – develop a thread which has the Templar tradition morphing into the beginnings of Freemasonry. As part of their argument, they cite the architectural wonder that is Rosslyn Chapel, built in the period 1440–1480. A prominent setting in Dan Brown's *The Da Vinci Code*, this small chapel is filled with esoteric and pagan symbols carved into every spare section of wall and ceiling. Curiously, there are also some motifs that some say give indications of an early manifestation of Freemasonry. For example, one of three heads carved in the ceiling, with head wound clearly visible, is referred to as the 'Widow's Son', a standard Masonic appellation first given to the Master Mason Hiram. The two beautifully carved pillars within the chapel are another echo of Masonic symbolism, that of the twin pillars of Jachin and Boaz. Also, according to *The Second Messiah* – the sequel to Lomas and Knight's *The Hiram Key* – Rosslyn was actually built to be a replica of the Jerusalem Temple.

In *The Second Messiah*, Knight and Lomas also stumbled over what they believe is another astonishing discovery. After a detailed inspection of the carvings at Rosslyn, they came across one that seems to illustrate perfectly a certain stage of the initiation rite for a candidate in Freemasonry.[26] This was a startling revelation, as it was evidence of a Masonic rite some two centuries before the first recorded initiation. Even more surprising was the fact that the person doing the initiation had a cross on the front of his robe – a Templar. Linking Masonry with the Templars and Essenes, Knight and Lomas believe that Rosslyn Chapel was in fact built to house the Essene scrolls, which they think were found by the Templars in Jerusalem:

> *The obvious was starting to descend upon us and we both had a simultaneous attack of goose pimples. Rosslyn was not a simple chapel; it was a post-Templar shrine built to house the scrolls found by Hugues de Payen and his team under the Holy of Holies of the last Temple at Jerusalem! Beneath our feet was the most priceless treasure in Christendom.*[27]

They state their opinion that William St Clair, builder of Rosslyn Chapel, secreted the treasure and then left coded instructions in the Holy Royal Arch degree of Masonry. Referring to the possible outline of a Seal of Solomon in the floor-plan of the chapel (which Dan Brown employed in *The Da Vinci Code*), they point at this Masonic definition of the instantly recognizable hexagram shape:

> *The Companion's Jewel of the Royal Arch is a double triangle, sometimes called the Seal of Solomon, within a circle of gold; at the bottom is a scroll bearing the words, 'Nil nisi clavis deest'* – *"Nothing but the key is wanting".*[28]

Whether Knight and Lomas are correct is still not known. Masonic historians of the calibre of Robert Cooper and Jay

Kinney have taken issue with a number of their claims (in *The Rosslyn Hoax?* and *The Masonic Myth*, respectively). However, Dan Brown certainly used the idea to his advantage in *The Da Vinci Code*, indicating that the 'Holy Grail' was hidden by the Seal of Solomon on the floor of Rosslyn Chapel. Dan Brown even cites the Royal Arch Degree in *The Da Vinci Code*, in a passage where Langdon describes the use of *la clef de voûte* (the key to the vault). He draws directly on the research of Knight and Lomas by describing this key as the central, wedge-shaped stone at the top of an arch which locks the pieces together and carries all the weight. And perhaps gives access to a secret chamber...

Baigent and Leigh argue that Rosslyn Chapel is evidence that the Templar tradition became ensconced in the 'safe haven' of Scotland after the suppression by Philippe IV of France, through a transfer to the secret initiations of Masonry. It is interesting to note other evidence that the Craft already existed around this time. For example, *The Templar Revelation* cites the evidence of an alchemical treatise dating to the 1450s – the same time frame as the construction of Rosslyn Chapel – which explicitly uses the term 'Freemason'.[29] Baigent and Leigh also refer to a manuscript from 1410 regarding a stonemason's guild, which mentions the "king's son of Tyre" and connects him with an ancient science from before the Great Flood, which was preserved in the teachings of Pythagoras and Hermes.[30]

According to *The Temple and the Lodge*, the Craft entered England proper in 1603 when the Scottish King James VI was crowned King of England, and Scottish aristocrats – the keepers of Masonry – moved south with their master. Again, it is pertinent to note the chronology, this being the exact time that both Francis Bacon and the Rosicrucian manifestos began coming to the fore.

Rosicrucians to Freemasons

What links can be found between the Rosicrucian philosophy and Freemasonry? Firstly, like the Utopian dream of the Rosicrucians – and appearing as a major theme in *The Lost Symbol* – the Craft promotes the doctrine that all men are brothers, who should be united in religious devotion to a higher being simply referred to as the 'Great Architect of the Universe'. In one of Freemasonry's guiding works, the *Book of Constitutions*, this is pronounced in the following manner:

> A Mason is oblig'd, by his Tenure, to obey the Moral Law; and if he rightly understands the Art, he will never be a stupid Atheist, nor an irreligious Libertine...'tis now thought more expedient only to oblige...to that Religion in which all Men agree, leaving their particular Opinions to themselves; that is, to be good Men and true, or Men of Honour and Honesty, by whatever Denominations or Persuasions they may be distinguish'd.[31]

The rules of the Mason's lodge include restricted discussion of both religion and politics, in order to help attain this goal – and perhaps as a method of easing the minds of the religious and secular authorities. Despite this professed avoidance of politics, however, Freemasonry has regularly played a part in democratic revolutions and interventions over the centuries – for example, in France, Mexico and Italy, and as we shall see in the United States as well. This may well be related back to the Utopian desire first professed by the Rosicrucian tradition.

In the way of more concrete evidence, a light-hearted poem published at Edinburgh in 1638 directly links the two organizations. Remember, this is only two decades after the appearance of the Rosicrucian tracts and eighty years before the official inauguration of the Grand Lodge in London. Written by Henry Adamson of Perth, the poem reads:

> *For what we do presage is not in grosse,*
> *For we be brethren of the Rosie Crosse:*
> *We have the Mason word and second sight,*
> *Things for to come we can foretell aright...*[32]

Some researchers believe that evidence for an early form of Freemasonry can be found in the work of artists such as the early 16th century painter and engraver Albrecht Dürer – a fact that Dan Brown seized upon in *The Lost Symbol*. Masonic symbols, such as the compass and 'memento mori' skull, can clearly be seen in some of his works. In his *Encyclopedia of Freemasonry*, Masonic authority Albert Mackey says that in Dürer's 1514 engraving *Melencolia I* we see "an exposition of medieval Freemasonry which suggests that [he] was familiar with the Fraternity of his time." This is the same engraving which features the 'magic square' which Dan Brown used so effectively in the plot of *The Lost Symbol* (a topic we'll return to in a later chapter).

In 1824 an essay appeared in *London Magazine* titled "Historico-Critical Inquiry into the Origins of the Rosicrucians and the Freemasons". The author, Thomas de Quincey, makes clear his belief that "no college or lodge of Rosicrucian brethren...can be shown from historical records to have ever been established". However, he does believe that the influence of the Rosicrucian manifestos inspired the creation of secret societies such as Freemasonry:

> *The original Free-Masons were a society that arose out of the Rosicrucian mania, certainly within the thirteen years from 1633 to 1646, and probably between 1633 and 1640.*[33]

Both de Quincey and Adamson mark a time frame that we covered in an earlier chapter – a decade after the publication of Sir Francis Bacon's *The New Atlantis* when the Utopians were petitioning the English parliament. If we look closely we see perhaps a hint that men like Samuel Hartlib were already involved in Masonry. In 1640 he wrote of his desire that the parliament "will lay the *cornerstone* of the worlds happinesse" – an explicitly Masonic term. The idea of a cornerstone as signifying the beginnings of a new construction are a potent symbol in Freemasonry, and Hartlib's choice of metaphor could well be an indication of a secret affiliation. So we may then also ask about the affiliations of Robert Boyle, as in 1647 he remarks in a letter "that the *cornerstones* of the Invisible…College, do now and then honor me with their company."

If so, he would not be the only member of the 'Invisible College' to be a card-carrying Freemason. In *The Rosicrucian Enlightenment,* Frances Yates points out that two of the earliest recorded initiations into speculative Masonry were also in the 1640s. One was Robert Moray, a major influence behind the establishment of the Royal Society in 1660, who was inducted into the mason's lodge of Edinburgh in May 1641. Five years later it is recorded that the alchemist and antiquarian Elias Ashmole, another of the foundation members of the Royal Society, became a Mason at a lodge in Lancashire.[34]

The name of the lodge in Lancashire where Ashmole was received is revealing: the 'House of Solomon'.[35] Here we find direct evidence that the Freemasons of the time were heavily influenced by Sir Francis Bacon's Utopian myth, *The New Atlantis,* remembering that the priests of the 'House of Solomon' on the Utopian island were the equivalent of the Rosicrucians. And Bacon's secret society may have been directly linked with the Templar tradition.

Another member of the Royal Society was, perhaps, the Rosicrucian adept *par excellence*: Sir Isaac Newton. As discussed in *The Lost Symbol*, not only did Newton discover some of the fundamental laws of nature – through rational, scientific investigation – but he also was fascinated with the spiritual aspect of life. In the words of Masonic historian Steven Bullock, Newton "drank deeply from the mysteries of alchemy and biblical prophecy even as he forged many of the concepts that underlay the later mechanistic science." For Newton and his peers in the 17th century, the ultimate goal was to recover the wisdom of the ancient world and to institute a new Golden Age upon Earth.

While the 'English experiment' dissolved with the advent of the civil war, the Utopian ideal of a brotherhood united in the quest for illumination of the ancient mysteries continued through the Royal Society, and ultimately Freemasonry. A century later, on the other side of the globe, a group of Freemasons may have begun a second experiment which would change the world…

CHAPTER 3

THE MASONIC FOUNDATIONS OF AMERICA

In 1897, an American army officer named Charles Totten wrote "there are mysteries connected with the birth of this Republic."[36] Totten had been investigating the strange iconography of the Great Seal of the United States, and through his research became convinced that the birth of the American nation could be related to the vision of Francis Bacon's *The New Atlantis*, who provided some financial support for the early Virginia colony. Totten's remark is, surprisingly, somewhat of an understatement.

On the 18th September, 1793, President George Washington took part in a Masonic ceremony to officially mark the beginning of the construction of the Capitol in Washington, D.C. Wearing his own Masonic apron, the first President of the United States of America marched to the site with the members of a number of local Freemasonry lodges, and then descended into the construction pit which housed the cornerstone of the building. Washington placed a silver plate upon the cornerstone, and then made the standard Masonic 'offerings' of corn, wine and oil. The Masonic tools carried by Washington on this momentous day are still held at a lodge in the District of Columbia.[37]

To many of us today, it seems strange that such an important day in the history of the United States of America would have such an overtly Masonic theme. What sort of importance did Freemasonry have in the founding of the United States? As it turns out, it seems to have been a highly significant factor.

Additionally, in *The Lost Symbol*, Dan Brown has Peter Solomon noting that many of the Founding Fathers were also Deist and Utopian in their philosophy:

> *"My friends, don't get me wrong, our forefathers were deeply religious men, but they were Deists—men who believed in God, but in a universal and open-minded way. The only religious ideal they put forth was religious freedom."* He

Masonic Procession During Capitol Cornerstone Ceremony

pulled the microphone from the podium and strode out to the edge of the stage. "*America's forefathers had a vision of a spiritually enlightened utopia, in which freedom of thought, education of the masses, and scientific advancement would replace the darkness of outdated religious superstition.*"

In *The Lost Symbol*, Dan Brown touches on this relationship between Freemasonry, Deism, and Utopian thought, and how it influenced the Founding Fathers – but curiously, he does not go into much detail. In previous chapters, we've already noted how the Rosicrucian tradition explains the links between these intertwined philosophies, and in this chapter, we'll discuss their impact on the Founding Fathers of the United States.

The Search for Utopia

The idea that the United States may have been founded as a 'Masonic Republic' is not a new one. We have already seen that Charles Totten considered it in 1897. The esoteric author Manly P. Hall also claims in his book, *The Secret Destiny of America*, that Sir Francis Bacon himself decided that the Utopian dream could be realized in North America,[38] as does Jim Marrs in *Rule by Secrecy* – and both are authors that Dan Brown is familiar with.

In their book *Talisman*, authors Robert Bauval and Graham Hancock point out research by historian Ron Heisler which suggests another link between Utopian visions in Europe and the new colony in America. Heisler discovered that the German occultist – and staunch Rosicrucian – Michael Maier was in close contact with a number of individuals connected with the Virginia Company. This group of wealthy individuals had been granted a royal charter by James I in 1606, basically giving them unlimited power of government in the colony. This charter had been drafted by none other than...Francis Bacon. Heisler believes that Maier's alchemical tract *Atalanta Fugiens* "may have been deeply inspired by the Utopian vision of America."

American scholar Donald R. Dickson provides another link between the Utopian dreamers and the Virginian settlement in his book *The Tessera of Antilia*. Dickson's investigations uncovered the existence of a Utopian society known as 'Antilia', which counted Rosicrucian instigator Valentin Andreae among its participants. Inspired by both the Rosicrucian tracts as well as Francis Bacon's writings, this brotherhood at one point contemplated emigrating *en masse* to Virginia in order to found their Utopian society.

It is clear then that some Utopian thinkers in Europe saw the Virginia colony as an ideal location for a 'new beginning'. In *The Temple and the Lodge,* Michael Baigent and Richard Leigh – the authors who provided the anagram for Leigh Teabing's name in *The Da Vinci Code* – also mention that according to some traditions, a form of Freemasonry arrived in the New World two decades before Bacon even published *The New Atlantis,* and actively worked to promote the Utopian society dreamed of by Rosicrucian thinkers.[39]

ENLIGHTENED RELIGION OF THE SUPREME ARCHITECT

At the turn of the 17th century, a revolution of thought was underway. As Rosicrucian thinking led to the flowering of the Royal Society in England, more and more thinkers across Europe took to Sir Francis Bacon's philosophy of basing knowledge on observation and experience. Isaac Newton stood at the crest of this new wave, and in the process discovered some of the fundamental laws of nature. And philosophers such as John Locke wrote tracts arguing that reasoned, scientific thinking, rather than faith in religious dogma, should be used in determining belief in a God.

From this burst of rationality, the school of religious thought known as Deism came forth. The core of Deist philosophy is that there *is* a God – or rather a 'Supreme Architect' – who created the Earth and human life, but that the Creator then withdrew from its creation to let it unfold without interference, as a watchmaker might construct and set in motion a watch, never to touch it again. As such, Deists did not generally believe in any of the miracles or supernatural events recounted in the Bible – instead, they saw God in the precise harmony of nature and its laws. In Thomas Paine's words: "The word of God is the creation we behold."

In France, the writings of the *philosophes* challenged traditional ideas of religion and government, and would make a deep impression on young minds in America during the 18th century – such as those of Franklin, Jefferson and Washington. Leading thinkers such as Voltaire and Diderot eviscerated organized religion not only for its irrational beliefs, but also for encouraging sectarian divisions and intolerance between opposing groups. Likewise, they challenged the tyranny of contemporary monarchies and governments, inflaming revolutionary feelings in both Europe and the Americas. There can hardly be any more succinct statement of the *zeitgeist* than the inflammatory words of Diderot: "Let us strangle the last king with the guts of the last priest!"

It can hardly be any surprise then that a number of the leading thinkers of the 18th century held common interests in Freemasonry, Utopianism and Deism. But in Freemasonry we find an additional thread of thought – the fascination with the ancient world and the idea that there was a 'purer wisdom' in those times which had been lost. This was a continuation of the 'underground tradition' that revered the wisdom of the ancients and which first arose during the occult revival of the early Renaissance and subsequent Rosicrucian Enlightenment.

In any case, the first documented Freemason to settle in the United States was a Scotsman by the name of John Skene. Initiated at a lodge in Aberdeen sometime before 1671, Skene settled in the New World in 1682, going on to become deputy governor of New Jersey. However, there are no records of a lodge in the United States prior to the formation of the Grand Lodge in London in 1717. What is interesting though, is that the first documented evidence referring to Freemasonry in America was printed in *The Pennsylvania Gazette* in 1730 – by one Benjamin Franklin.

Benjamin Franklin

Few people could claim to possess the talents of Dr Benjamin Franklin. A journalist and author, he published and wrote for his own newspaper, *The Pennsylvania Gazette*, during the first half of the 18th century. With a group of like-minded individuals, he also founded Pennsylvania's first library in 1732 and devoted himself to the spread of knowledge and learning.

Franklin is also widely known for his scientific work and inventions, with his famous experiment of flying a kite during a storm (to demonstrate that lightning was a form of electricity) becoming part of popular folklore. To complement his reputation as one of the great scientists of the 18th century, he also invented two common devices still used today – the lightning rod and bifocal spectacles. He therefore stands firmly in the tradition of Newton and other members of the Royal Society, and his discoveries made a significant impact upon religious thought at the time.

In his book *A History of the Warfare of Science with Theology*, Andrew Dickson White says that Franklin's research into lightning was a "death-blow" to religious theories about the influence of God upon the weather; "at the moment when he drew the electric spark from the cloud, the whole tremendous fabric of theological meteorology reared by the fathers, the popes, the mediaeval doctors, and the long line of great theologians, Catholic and Protestant, collapsed":

> *The older Church, while clinging to the old theory, was finally obliged to confess the supremacy of Franklin's theory practically; for his lightning-rod did what exorcisms, and holy water, and processions, and the Agnus Dei, and the ringing of church bells, and the rack, and the burning of witches, had failed to do. This was clearly seen, even by the poorest peasants in eastern France, when they observed that the grand spire of Strasburg Cathedral, which neither the sacredness of the place, nor the bells within it, nor the holy water and relics beneath it, could protect from frequent injuries by lightning, was once and for all protected by Franklin's rod.*

Franklin was also a diplomat and power-broker who was of profound importance to the founding of the United States. His role in discussions between England and the colonies on various matters began in the 1750s, making the suggestion of a union of the colonies as far back as 1754. In 1765, when the British Parliament passed the infamous Stamp Act (a tax levy on a wide variety of documents in the American colonies, which was a trigger for the separatist movement that led to the American Revolution), Franklin actively opposed it. In 1775 he was elected a member of the Continental Congress, and played a key role in the Declaration of Independence, despite his personal preference to remain affiliated with the British empire.

Franklin was posted as the new nation's diplomat to France in 1776, and conducted his role with great success. He was instrumental in securing a military alliance with France, and negotiated the peace with Great Britain via the Treaty of Paris in 1783. He is the only Founding Father who is a signatory to the three foundation documents of the United States: the Declaration of Independence, the Treaty of Paris and the United States Constitution.

Benjamin Franklin was also a Freemason and a Deist, though it must be said that his Deism was of the 'soft' variety. For example, he wrote in the 1730s that God "sometimes interferes by His particular providence," contrary to the Deist view that God withdrew from the world immediately after the creation, never to intervene. Nevertheless, he still pointed out some of the hypocrisies and false thinking that dogged orthodox religious views. "Sin is not hurtful because it is forbidden," he wrote in 1739, "but it is forbidden because it is hurtful." Similarly, he elegantly dismembered the religiosity of many people in saying that "serving God is doing good to man, but praying is thought an easier service and therefore is more generally chosen."[40]

Given the latter aphorism, it is not surprising that Franklin was attracted to the Brotherhood – the fraternity shared his dedication to fellowship, civil works and nonsectarian religious tolerance. He was initiated into Freemasonry in February 1731, and rose to the rank of Provincial Grand Master of Pennsylvania by 1734 (while still in his 20s), going on to become Provincial Grand Master of the colonies in 1749. As a publisher, he was in a unique position to aid the cause of Freemasonry in the New World. He published Anderson's *Book of Constitutions,* the authoritative Masonic document, in 1734. In 1756 he had been inducted into the Royal Society in England, which we have seen was heavily Masonic and perhaps Rosicrucian in nature.[41] And in 1778, while in France, he was initiated into the highly influential 'Neuf Soeurs' ('Nine

Sisters') lodge in Paris, which would boast Voltaire, Lafayette, Court de Gebelin and numerous instigators of the French Revolution as members.[42] He was also a friend of the Englishman Sir Francis Dashwood – founder of the Hellfire Club.

Franklin was involved in a 'quasi-Masonic' controversy in 1737, when a naïve apprentice named Daniel Rees who desired to join the Freemasons was killed as a consequence of a practical joke gone wrong. Walter Isaacson, in his excellent biography *Benjamin Franklin: An American Life*, recounts the sordid tale:

> *A gang of rowdy acquaintances, not Freemasons, sought to have sport with him and concocted a ritual filled with weird oaths, purgatives, and butt kissing. When they told Franklin of their prank, he laughed and asked for a copy of the fake oaths. A few days later, the hooligans enacted another ceremony, where the hapless Rees was accidentally burned to death by a bowl of flaming brandy. Franklin was not involved, but was called as a witness in the subsequent manslaughter trial.*

Franklin's publishing rivals gleefully pounced on the news that he was associated in some way with the controversy, and word of his involvement spread throughout the colonies. His parents were distressed at not only his link to this particular case, but to his membership of Freemasonry as well. In a letter to his father, Franklin sought to allay his mother's fears about the Fraternity – while acknowledging that she had every right to dislike the Brotherhood on the basis of their exclusion of women. But, Franklin pleaded, "I must entreat her to suspend her judgement till she is better informed, unless she will believe me, when I assure her that they are in general a very harmless sort of people, and have no principles or practices that are inconsistent with religion and good manners."

Moving from Benjamin Franklin's rather mundane view of Freemasonry to something more exciting (if not a little speculative), we should note that Manly P. Hall, in *The Secret Destiny of America*, claims – with barely circumstantial evidence, it must be said – that Benjamin Franklin was part of the 'Order of the Quest', the secret movement to construct a Utopian democracy in the New World:

> *Men bound by a secret oath to labor in the cause of world democracy decided that in the American colonies they would plant the roots of a new way of life...Benjamin Franklin exercised an enormous psychological influence in Colonial politics as the appointed spokesman of the unknown philosophers; he did not make laws, but his words became law.*

Given that Dan Brown is more than familiar with the books of Manly Hall (he is referenced twice in *The Lost Symbol*), it is surprising that he did not use this 'Order of the Quest' material in the new book – it seems tailor-made to a fiction novel concerning the secret history of America!

Franklin's religious tolerance offers the ultimate reinforcement of the message of *The Lost Symbol*, and of Freemasonry, that all religions are ultimately one and we are a brotherhood of man. During his life, Franklin contributed to the construction budgets of every church in Philadelphia, as well as the one and only synagogue. Upon his death in 1790, almost 20,000 people observed his funeral procession, while at the front of the cortege marched "the clergymen of the city, all of them, of every faith."[43]

Benjamin Franklin had been a Freemason for almost fifty years by the time he signed the Declaration of Independence. What other Masonic influences can we find in the founding of the United States?

George Washington

As we have already noted above, George Washington was most definitely a Freemason. The commander-in-chief of the colonial armies during the American Revolutionary War was initiated into the lodge at Fredericksburg on the 4th of November 1752. Interestingly, he became an Entered Apprentice in the Craft before his 21st birthday, in contradiction of guidelines that initiations not occur until the applicant is "of mature age". Some have explained away the anomaly based on his appearance – Washington was a huge man, standing 6 feet two inches in height. Perhaps the most likely explanation though was offered by Joseph Eggleston in his *Masonic Life of Washington*, who suggested that the change from the Julian calendar to the Gregorian calendar – which had occurred just two months previous – had confused officials:

> *Many of his biographers state his birth as having occurred February 11, Old Style, 1731-2, and doubtless the record being 1731, no one even thought of counting up the elapsed time, but all assumed that he was over twenty-one.*

In any case, Washington was 'raised' as a Master Mason only a year later. In 1777 he was offered the position of Grand Master of the planned Grand Lodge of the United States, but he declined (quite ironically) on the basis that he was not qualified for such a high office.[44]

There is little doubt that Washington would have been more than capable of filling this position – his refusal to accept was based more on a genuine modesty which remained in evidence throughout his life. He refused to be paid for his military service, and left the room when John Adams recommended him for the position of commander-in-chief of the Continental Army. Despite accepting the post, Washington told the Continental Congress

1794 portrait of George Washington wearing Masonic jewel and apron

that he was unworthy of the honor. He was also reluctant to be seen using his power as President of the United States. Thomas Jefferson wrote of him:

> *The moderation and virtue of a single character probably prevented this Revolution from being closed, as most others have been, by a subversion of that liberty it was intended to establish.*

In 1788, the year before becoming the first President of the United States, Washington did become Master of the Alexandria lodge in Washington, D.C., today known as the Alexandria Washington Lodge No. 22. The lodge became the site of the George Washington Masonic Memorial in 1932, a huge Masonic landmark modeled on the ancient Lighthouse of Alexandria in Egypt, the 'Pharos', which played a small cameo part in *The Lost Symbol*.

Despite attending church services with his wife, Washington held philosophical and religious views which suggest that he, like Franklin, was a Deist. As religious scholar David L. Holmes points out, "Washington was more concerned with morality and ethics than with adhering to the doctrines of a particular church. He seemed to have no interest in theology." Washington would regularly leave services before communion, a habit which moved the Reverend Dr. James Abercrombie to compose a sermon scolding those in high positions for setting a bad example with their church attendance. Washington responded by ceasing to turn up at all – probably not exactly the response Reverend Abercrombie was looking for! In his speeches and letters, Washington rarely mentioned Christianity and Jesus Christ, and when referring to God often substituted the terms "Supreme Ruler of the Universe", "Author of all Good", and the Masonic "Grand Architect". More plainly, when Reverend Abercrombie was asked about Washington's religious views later in life, he simply replied: "Sir, Washington was a Deist."

Washington died on December 14, 1799, with his friend and Masonic brother Dr. Elisha Dick in attendance. As he approached his final moments, Washington – who had a particular fear of false burial – had requested that his body not be put "into the vault in less than three days after I am dead." And despite requests for his body to be interred in the crypt of the Capitol, and later at the Washington Monument, his wife Martha honored his request to lie in peace in the family crypt at Mount Vernon. Dr. Dick performed the Masonic funeral service which took place on December 18, with the brothers of Alexandria Lodge No. 22 in attendance. He placed Washington's Masonic apron in the coffin, followed by a sprig of acacia, the Masonic symbol for immortality.

If all that seems a bit too mundane, perhaps you'd prefer the version recounted in Mason Locke Weems' book *A History of the Life and Death, Virtues and Exploits of General George Washington*. Not afraid to dress things up a little, Weems told how the recently-departed, saintly spirit of George Washington ascended on angel's wings…

> …*while voices more than human were warbling through the happy regions, and hymning the great procession towards the gates of heaven. His glorious coming was seen afar off; and myriads of mighty angels hastened forth, with golden harps, to welcome the honoured stranger.*

While the prose may have been a vibrant purple color, it did echo the sentiments of the nation. To many, George Washington was a saint – to some even an American deity. Weems' descriptive death scene was echoed in engravings by David Edwin in 1800, and John James Barralet in 1816, both under the title *The Apotheosis of*

Barralet's "Commemoration/Apotheosis of Washington"

Brumidi's "Apotheosis of Washington" in the Capitol dome

George Washington. These images reached their...er, apotheosis... with Constantino Brumidi's famous fresco within the dome of the Capitol, completed in 1865 – now brought firmly into the eye of the general public through Dan Brown's *The Lost Symbol*.

Thomas Jefferson

All the available evidence suggests that Thomas Jefferson was not a Freemason, although he did agree with the philosophy of the Craft and was a confirmed Deist. He created his own personal Bible from the New Testament, by omitting supernatural sections and leaving only the philosophical teachings. This unique compilation became known as the 'Jefferson Bible' – in the early 1900s approximately 2500 copies were printed for the United States Congress.[45]

While historians point out that there is no evidence to tie Thomas Jefferson officially to any Masonic organization, it is a matter of fact that he had great sympathy for the cause. In a letter to Bishop James Madison in 1800, Jefferson relayed his thoughts on Adam Weishaupt and his Illuminati (not to be confused with the fictional Illuminati of Dan Brown's *Angels and Demons*). In what amounts to a defense of both Masonry and Weishaupt's Illuminati, against the conspiracy charges laid by the writers Barruel and Robison, Jefferson's allegiances clearly lie with the Utopian and Masonic ideals rather than Church and State. His words also echo one of the major themes of *The Lost Symbol*, that of each individual looking within and improving themselves:

> *[Weishaupt] is among those…who believe in the indefinite perfectibility of man. He thinks he may in time be rendered so perfect that he will be able to govern himself in every circumstance so as to injure none, to do all the good he can, to leave government no occasion to exercise their powers over him…Weishaupt believes that to promote this perfection of the human character was the object of Jesus Christ. That his intention was simply to reinstate natural religion, and by diffusing the light of his morality, to teach us to govern ourselves. His precepts are the love of god & love of our neighbor. And by teaching innocence of conduct, he expected to place men in their natural state of liberty and equality. He says, no one ever laid a surer foundation for liberty than our grand master, Jesus of Nazareth. He believes the Free Masons were originally possessed of the true principles and objects of Christianity, and have still preserved some of them by tradition, but much disfigured.*
>
> *…As Weishaupt lived under the tyranny of a despot and priests, he knew that caution was necessary even in spreading information, and the principles of pure morality. He proposed*

therefore to lead the Free masons to adopt this object and to make the objects of their institution the diffusion of science & virtue...

This has given an air of mystery to his views, was the foundation of his banishment, the subversion of the Masonic order, and is the colour for the ravings against him of Robison, Barruel and Morse, whose real fears are that the craft would be endangered by the spreading of information, reason and natural morality among men...if Weishaupt had written here, where no secrecy is necessary in our endeavors to render men wise and virtuous, he would not have thought of any secret machinery for that purpose.[46]

In his excellent book *The Faiths of the Founding Fathers*, David L. Holmes points out that Jefferson's religious viewpoint could best be described as "restorationist", and his description of this term is certainly in keeping with Dan Brown's theme in *The Lost Symbol*:

In all fields, restorationists attempt to restore a lost set of truths. Christian restorationists believe in a golden era... from which the church has fallen away...Jefferson came to believe that the combined effect of power-hungry monarchs and corrupt 'priests' had despoiled the original, pristine teachings of Jesus.

Jefferson was the primary author of the Declaration of Independence, and as well as being the third President of the United States also served at various times as Vice-President, Secretary of State and ambassador to France. During his travels to France he accompanied his good friend Benjamin Franklin to the 'Nine Sisters' Masonic lodge, and many of his closest associates and confidantes were Freemasons.

Thomas Paine

Thomas Paine is yet another Founding Father who held strong Deist views. Born and bred in England, Paine didn't move to the colonies until his late thirties, only a matter of years before the Declaration of Independence. He emigrated on the advice of Benjamin Franklin, whom he had met in London. Barely a year after arriving, he published the massively influential *Common Sense* on January 10th 1776, which is said to have sold more than 600,000 copies in a population of only three million. His words inspired George Washington to seek the route of independence from Great Britain, and Thomas Jefferson partly based the Declaration of Independence upon them. Paine also has the honor of being the person to suggest the name of the United States of America.[47]

This revolutionary thinker was sentenced *in absentia* in Great Britain for sedition, and despite his support for the French Revolution in his *Rights of Man,* was imprisoned and sentenced to death by the revolutionaries for arguing against the execution of Louis XVI. Miraculously, he escaped the guillotine when the executioner marked his door incorrectly,[48] finally gaining his freedom via the pleas of the new American Minister to France (and future President of the United States), James Monroe – who was also a Freemason.

Many Americans would be surprised to know that the man who coined the name of the United States, and had such a profound impact upon its independence, had strong feelings against Christianity. Unlike Franklin, who was exceptionally tolerant of religious views that differed from his own, Paine derided Christianity as "a fable, which, for absurdity and extravagance is not exceeded by any thing that is to be found in the mythology of the ancients." In his *Age of Reason* Paine wrote:

> *The opinions I have advanced…are the effect of the most clear and long-established conviction that the Bible and the Testament are impositions upon the world, that the fall of man, the account of Jesus Christ being the Son of God, and of his dying to appease the wrath of God, and of salvation by that strange means, are all fabulous inventions, dishonorable to the wisdom and power of the Almighty; that the only true religion is Deism, by which I then meant, and mean now, the belief of one God, and an imitation of his moral character, or the practice of what are called moral virtues.*[49]

Instead, Paine advocated Deism, declaring it superior to Christianity: "It believes in God, and there it rests," Paine wrote. "It honours Reason as the choicest gift of God to man and the faculty by which he is enabled to contemplate the power, wisdom, and goodness of the Creator displayed in the creation."

There is no direct evidence that Paine was a Freemason. However, after his death a posthumous essay was published, titled "The Origins of Freemasonry". Whatever his official status was, Paine certainly seems to have had access to information about the Craft:

> *The Entered Apprentice knows but little more of Masonry than the use of signs and tokens, and certain steps and words by which Masons can recognize each other without being discovered by a person who is not a Mason. The Fellow Craft is not much better instructed in Masonry, than the Entered Apprentice. It is only in the Master Mason's Lodge, that whatever knowledge remains of the origin of Masonry is preserved and concealed.*[50]

Paine was an equal opportunity debunker of myth though, and wasn't afraid to point out what seemed to him to be a glaring error in the legend of Masonry:

> *The original institution of Masonry consisted in the foundation of the liberal arts and sciences, but more especially in Geometry, for at the building of the tower of Babel, the art and mystery of Masonry was first introduced, and from thence handed down by Euclid, a worthy and excellent mathematician of the Egyptians; and he communicated it to Hiram, the Master Mason concerned in building Solomon's Temple in Jerusalem.*
>
> *Besides the absurdity of deriving Masonry from the building of Babel, where, according to the story, the confusion of languages prevented the builders understanding each other, and consequently of communicating any knowledge they had, there is a glaring contradiction in point of chronology in the account he gives.*
>
> *Solomon's Temple was built and dedicated 1004 years before the Christian era; and Euclid, as may be seen in the tables of chronology, lived 277 before the same era. It was therefore impossible that Euclid could communicate any thing to Hiram, since Euclid did not live till 700 years after the time of Hiram.*[51]

Paine believed that Masonry had a different origin than is stated in the myths of the Craft. He promoted his own view that Freemasonry was derived from the remnants of the Druidic religion, which was the most recent culture to bear a line of mystical knowledge which also passed through the hands of the Romans, Greeks, Egyptians and Chaldeans. And ultimately, according to Paine, Masonry was based on the worship of the heavens, and in particular, the Sun.

One of Paine's friends, the revolutionist Nicolas de Bonneville – who also counted Benjamin Franklin as a friend – was even more explicit on the Egyptian origins of modern religions and movements. In his book *De L'Esprit des Religion*, published in 1791, de Bonneville claimed that Christian religion itself stemmed from the ancient cult of Isis.[52] It has often been pointed out that statues of the Virgin Mary and baby Jesus bear a close resemblance to the Egyptian sculptures of Isis and the child Horus.

Paine claimed that the veil of secrecy which Masons worked under was in order to avoid persecution by the religion which took over the worship of the Sun – Christianity:

> *The natural source of secrecy is fear. When any new religion over-runs a former religion, the professors of the new become the persecutors of the old. We see this in all instances that history brings before us…when the Christian religion over-ran the religion of the Druids in Italy, ancient Gaul, Britain, and Ireland, the Druids became the subject of persecution. This would naturally and necessarily oblige such of them as remained attached to their original religion to meet in secret, and under the strongest injunctions of secrecy…from the remains of the religion of the Druids, thus preserved, arose the institution which, to avoid the name of Druid, took that of Mason, and practiced under this new name the rites and ceremonies of Druids.*[53]

Paine's enmity against Christianity has meant that to a large extent, his role in the independence of the United States has been swept under the proverbial carpet (some ill-advised criticism of George Washington did not help his cause either). Theodore Roosevelt inaccurately called Paine "a dirty little atheist" (being a Deist, Paine did believe in a supreme being), and in 1925 Thomas Edison conceded that "if Paine had ceased his writings with *The Rights of Man* he would have been hailed today as one of the two or three outstanding figures of the Revolution…*The Age of Reason* cost him glory at the hands of his countrymen."[54]

Alexander Hamilton

Alexander Hamilton was certainly not blessed with an easy start in life. He was born in the West Indies as the illegitimate son of a struggling businessman from Scotland, James Hamilton, and Rachel Fawcett Lavien – who was at the time married to another man. His father abandoned him, and his mother died in his early teens. However, his precocious intellect and raw ambition paved the way for a meteoric rise: by the end of his teenage years, Hamilton was General George Washington's most trusted *aide-de-camp*, and a published pamphleteer of renown on the subjects of government and economics.

President George Washington appointed Hamilton as the United States' first Secretary of the Treasury, a post in which he served from 1789 until 1795. His tenure marked him as one of America's most important statesman, with some saying his financial and political genius paved the way for the United States to become the super-power it is today.

Despite his modest beginnings, Hamilton had a strong belief that only a 'chosen few' were fit to govern and that power should be centralized, once saying "ancient democracies in which the people themselves deliberated never possessed one good feature of government." His vision of the U.S. was for power to be taken away from the states and put in the hands of a central government. This clashed with the ideals of Thomas Jefferson, and the two were often at odds over the governing of the fledgling nation. Jefferson – known for his political paranoia – became convinced that Hamilton led a "corrupt squadron" who would destroy the good work done in creating the U.S. Constitution, by getting rid of the limitations it imposed on the government. Jefferson feared that Hamilton's vision would bring about "a change, from the present republican form of government, to that of a monarchy" – exactly the type of government that Utopians were desperate to free themselves from.

Hamilton also instigated the creation of the first national bank of the United States, once again meeting intense opposition from Jefferson, who was at the time the Secretary of State. One of Hamilton's more infamous quotes gives support to Jefferson's concerns about Hamilton's version of democracy:

> *All communities divide themselves into the few and the many. The first are the rich and the well-born; the other the mass of the people...turbulent and changing, they seldom judge or determine right. Give therefore to the first class a distinct, permanent share in the Government. Nothing but a permanent body can check the imprudence of democracy.*

There is some confusion as to whether Hamilton was a Freemason. 33rd Degree Mason Henry Clausen claims Hamilton as a 'Brother' in his book, *Masons Who Helped Shape Our Nation*, as does Gordon S. Wood in *The Radicalism of the American Revolution*. However, Masonic scholar Allen E. Roberts specifically states that Hamilton was not a Mason in his respected tome, *Freemasonry in American History*.

Hamilton's life came to a bizarre end on July 12, 1804. It is alleged that he privately made comments questioning the integrity of the third Vice-President of the United States, Aaron Burr – although this incident was more the final straw in a long-simmering antipathy between the two, with Hamilton previously causing serious injury to Burr's chances of becoming President. Burr demanded an apology for Hamilton's slight, but Hamilton refused – saying he could not recall making any such remarks. A duel was set to resolve the issue, with Burr and Hamilton coming together on a rocky ledge in Weehawken, New Jersey – the same place where Hamilton's son Phillip had been killed in a duel just three years previous. Burr shot and mortally wounded Hamilton, who died the next day.

Masons Everywhere

We have seen that a number of the Founding Fathers of the United States were ambivalent, if not downright hostile, towards Christianity. A strong thread of Deism runs through the ranks of the influential personalities involved in America's independence. But stronger still is the presence of Freemasonry. Not only were many of the Founding Fathers initiates of the Craft, but also numerous generals in the Continental Army, as well as other individuals who loom large in the drive for independence, such as the Frenchman Gilbert Lafayette.

This young idealistic French aristocrat took the position of Major-General in the Continental Army, with the request that he not be paid for his service, at the grand age of 19. His exemplary service for the fledgling United States earned him the respect of George Washington, whom he thereafter held as a life-long friend. Lafayette also spent time with Benjamin Franklin in Paris, where they were both members of the 'Nine Sisters' Masonic lodge – in fact, each supported an arm of the aged *philosophe* Voltaire as he was inducted into the influential organization. Lafayette's prominence in the Revolutionary War has led to approximately four hundred public places and streets in the United States being named after him.[55] It is said that when American troops liberated Paris in the First World War, Colonel C. E. Stanton – on behalf of the U.S. General John Perching, a 33rd Degree Freemason – stood before Lafayette's tomb on the 4th of July 1917, proclaiming "Lafayette, we are here!"[56]

One of the legendary moments in the move towards independence was the 'Boston Tea Party'. On the night of the 16th of December 1773, a group of Boston locals protesting the importation of duty-free tea from the East India Tea Company, boarded the merchant ship *Dartmouth* and dumped its entire cargo of tea into the harbor. While devoid of bloodshed, this incident marked the beginning of the Revolution, as it ignited colonial passions against the strictures and impositions of the parliament of Great Britain. What is unknown to many is that at least twelve members of the local Masonic lodge were involved in the Boston Tea Party – including the patriot Paul Revere – and at least another twelve of the participants subsequently joined it.

Another influential contributor to the drive for independence was a Jewish Freemason named Haym Solomon, who had amassed a fortune through his dealings as a banker and merchant. Solomon had a deep belief that the United States would go on to become a beacon of the world, and as such devoted not only his own fortune to the revolutionary cause, but also played a huge role in raising money from international sources – helped by his proficiency in eight languages.

Haym Solomon negotiated war aid from France and Holland, and acted as paymaster-general of the French military forces during the Revolutionary War. He is said to have loaned the fledgling government about $600,000, of which at least $400,000 was never repaid. He also financially assisted icons such as Jefferson and Madison, and was a close personal friend of George Washington.[57] Did Haym Solomon provide the blueprint for the character of 'Peter Solomon' in *The Lost Symbol*?

The list could go on. Benedict Arnold, the famous 'turncoat' of the American Revolution was a Freemason. Friedrich Wilhelm von Steuben was – like Lafayette – another foreigner and Freemason who ably assisted the American Revolutionaries. John Hancock, who is remembered often for his signature on the Declaration of Independence, was also a Mason. In fact, Masonic historian Steven C. Bullock wrote more than 300 pages on the influence of Freemasonry on Revolutionary America in his scholarly book *Revolutionary Brotherhood*. There can be little doubt, therefore, that Freemasonry was a prominent part of the lives of many of those responsible for the founding of the United States.

A Strange Tale

In his book *The Secret Destiny of America,* the respected esotericist Manly P. Hall recounts a bizarre piece of folklore regarding the creation of the American flag, and it bears retelling here.[58] Hall says he first came across the strange tale in the 1890 book *Our Flag, or the Evolution of the Stars and Stripes,* authored by Robert Alan Campbell. It tells how the Continental Congress met in 1775 to discuss the creation of a Colonial flag; Benjamin Franklin and George Washington were just two of the luminaries present.

Campbell states that the flag committee met at a house in Cambridge, Massachusetts, near where General Washington was encamped. Staying at this house was an old gentleman – referred to only as the 'Professor' – and due to space constraints Benjamin Franklin offered to share apartments with the enigmatic man. Little is known about the Professor, except that he was at least 70 years old, and he "ate no flesh, fish, nor fowl, or any green things, and drank no liquor, wine, or ale". He lived only on cereals, fruits and tea, and spent most of his time poring over ancient books and rare manuscripts.

When the Professor was introduced to the Continental Congress, Benjamin Franklin stepped forward and shook his hand. At this point, Campbell says, there was an obvious and mutual recognition between the two – perhaps indicative of a Masonic handshake or the like? In any case, after dinner Franklin exchanged a few words with Washington and the committee, and then made the curious move of asking the stranger to take part in the flag meeting.

On acceptance of the invitation, the Professor lost no time in asserting himself. He immediately recommended that the hostess be included as secretary of the committee, to increase the number of members from the inauspicious number of six to the more numerologically significant figure of seven – a suggestion that was unanimously accepted by the committee.

It was abundantly clear that this mysterious individual was well-grounded in numerology, as well as other ancient and mystical sciences such as astrology. Campbell quotes him as standing before the committee delivering this speech:

> *As the sun rises from his grave in Capricorn, mounts toward his resurrection in Aries and pass onward and upward to his glorious culmination in Cancer, so will our political sun rise and continue to increase in power, in light, and in glory; and the exalted sun of summer will not have gained his full strength of heat and power in the starry Lion until our Colonial Sun will be, in its glorious exaltation, demanding a place in the governmental firmaments alongside of, coordinate with, and in no wise subordinate to, any other sun of any other nation upon earth.*[59]

The Professor then recommended his design for the flag, which would allow for modification based on the upward rise of the United States. Campbell says that the committee approved this suggested design, and the flag was promptly adopted by George Washington as the standard for the Colonial Army.

Designing a Nation

Although it has often been claimed that up to 50 of the 56 signatories to the Declaration of Independence were

Freemasons, the 'official' number is put at between 8 and 15. While this may seem to quash the conspiracy theories, it is still a significant number, especially so when one considers that such influential personalities as Franklin and Washington were longtime Masons. Despite the modern-day belief of many that the United States is a nation built from a strong Christian base, in truth a number of its founders were non-Christian, and seem to have had a deep and abiding desire to create a new land where the tyrannies of religion and government – as seen in Europe – were largely kept in check.

Manly Hall's *The Secret Destiny of America* claims that the creation of the United States was the prime goal of the 'Order of the Quest', a secret society composed of intellectuals and philosophers which had survived from ancient times. Hall says that the American Revolution was a step towards the ultimate aim of a worldwide democracy:

> *All these groups [Knights of the Holy Grail, Christian and Jewish Cabalists, Rosicrucians, the Illuminati] belong to what is called The Order of the Quest. All were searching for one and the same thing under a variety of rituals and symbols. That one thing was a perfected social order, Plato's commonwealth, the government of the philosopher-king.*[60]

It must be said though, that this is *not* the view of orthodox historians. In actual fact, it is difficult to establish authoritatively whether or not secret societies guided colonial America towards a definite goal, or whether they only exercised an influence via the common philosophy shared by each of them – the ideal originally enunciated by Francis Bacon in *The New Atlantis*. No matter what the truth, Freemasonry most definitely played some sort of role in the creation of the new republic. Masonic historian

Ronald Heaton goes as far as to say that the Craft was more influential than any other institution in the establishment of the United States:

> *Neither general historians nor the members of the Fraternity since the days of the first Constitutional Conventions have realized how much the United States of America owes to Freemasonry, and how great a part it played in the birth of the nation and the establishment of the landmarks of that civilization.*[61]

Incidentally, Heaton's mention of the establishment of landmarks brings us to another of the major themes of *The Lost Symbol*: the esoteric architecture of Washington, D.C.

CHAPTER 4

STRANGE CONSTRUCTIONS

As we saw at the start of the last chapter, the beginning of construction work in the United States capital was heavily flavored with Masonic overtones. With local lodges presiding over cornerstone ceremonies, and the President himself being a Freemason, it would appear that the building of Washington, D.C. may have been strongly influenced by the culture of the Craft. That Dan Brown weaved this architecture into the plotline of *The Lost Symbol* is no great surprise – both of Brown's previous Robert Langdon novels used the art and architecture of well-known cities to good advantage. In *Angels and Demons* Langdon follows the 'Way of Light' marked by the sculptures of Bernini, with many other references to the architecture of Rome spread throughout the book. In *The Da Vinci Code,* Brown used the art of the Renaissance master Leonardo da Vinci, as well as some of the esoteric themes in Parisian architecture (and Rosslyn towards the end of the book).

Surprisingly, Dan Brown only revealed the tip of the iceberg when it comes to the hidden history of the capital. In some cases he barely mentions monuments which could have featured prominently – such as the George Washington Masonic Memorial – while at other times he portrays some fascinating aspects simply as the imagination of 'conspiracy theorists'. And there are a number of other locations worthy of inclusion which never made it into the pages of *The Lost Symbol*. Let's dig a little deeper.

Designing History

The site of Washington, D.C. was selected during a dinner between Thomas Jefferson and Alexander Hamilton, with Jefferson agreeing to support Hamilton's federal financial plans in exchange for land dedicated to a capital. The states of Virginia and Maryland donated the necessary land, and in 1790 the site was designated as the District of Columbia, with the capital taking its name from George Washington.

The city plan was originally designed by the Frenchman Pierre Charles L'Enfant, who had served in the Revolutionary War after arriving with Lafayette. Dan Brown claims in *The Lost Symbol* that L'Enfant was a Freemason, possibly referencing David Ovason's book about Washington, D.C., *The Sacred Architecture of Our Nation's Capital*, which is one of the few books to make this claim. However, Ovason's source for this claim is hardly rock-solid. "The discovery of the manuscript revealing this information has not yet been reported in the Masonic literature," Ovason remarks in the endnotes of his book. "[C]onsequently I do not feel free to reveal the source of this information, which came to me by way of private conversation." It might therefore be worth taking this particular claim with a grain of salt.

In any case, L'Enfant was dismissed from his position early on in the project due to personality conflicts. The emotional Frenchman took his design drawings with him when he left, but the plan was still reproduced reasonably faithfully from the memory of those who continued with the project. An astronomer and surveyor, Andrew Ellicott, took over from L'Enfant, with both Jefferson and Washington contributing ideas. On April 15, 1791, Dr. E. C. Dick, the Worshipful Master of Alexandria Lodge, No. 22, with the assistance of his Masonic brothers, laid the cornerstone of the District of Columbia – the stone being located, as per tradition, at the southeast corner of the Federal District, at Jones's Point.

Washington, D.C. is divided into four quadrants, marked by the cardinal directions, with the center point being the Capitol building. However, as the Capitol is not at the center of the district, the quadrants are unequal in size. L'Enfant's plan for Washington, D.C. includes many diagonal avenues which are named after the states, probably the most famous of which is Pennsylvania Avenue which connects the White House and the Capitol. In the original plan, the Capitol, the White House and the Washington Monument form a right-angled triangle.

As a side note, the White House used to be called the Presidential Mansion, until it was burned by the British during a raid in 1814 – along with the Capitol and the bridge across the Potomac. As a consequence, white paint was used to disguise the blackened walls, and from that point on it was referred to as the White House.

Washington and the Sacred Feminine

In *The Lost Symbol*, Dan Brown has Langdon explain to his class the importance of astrology on the starting date of construction of the Capitol building: "What if I told you that precise moment was chosen by three famous Masons – George Washington, Benjamin Franklin, and Pierre L'Enfant, the primary architect for D.C.?"

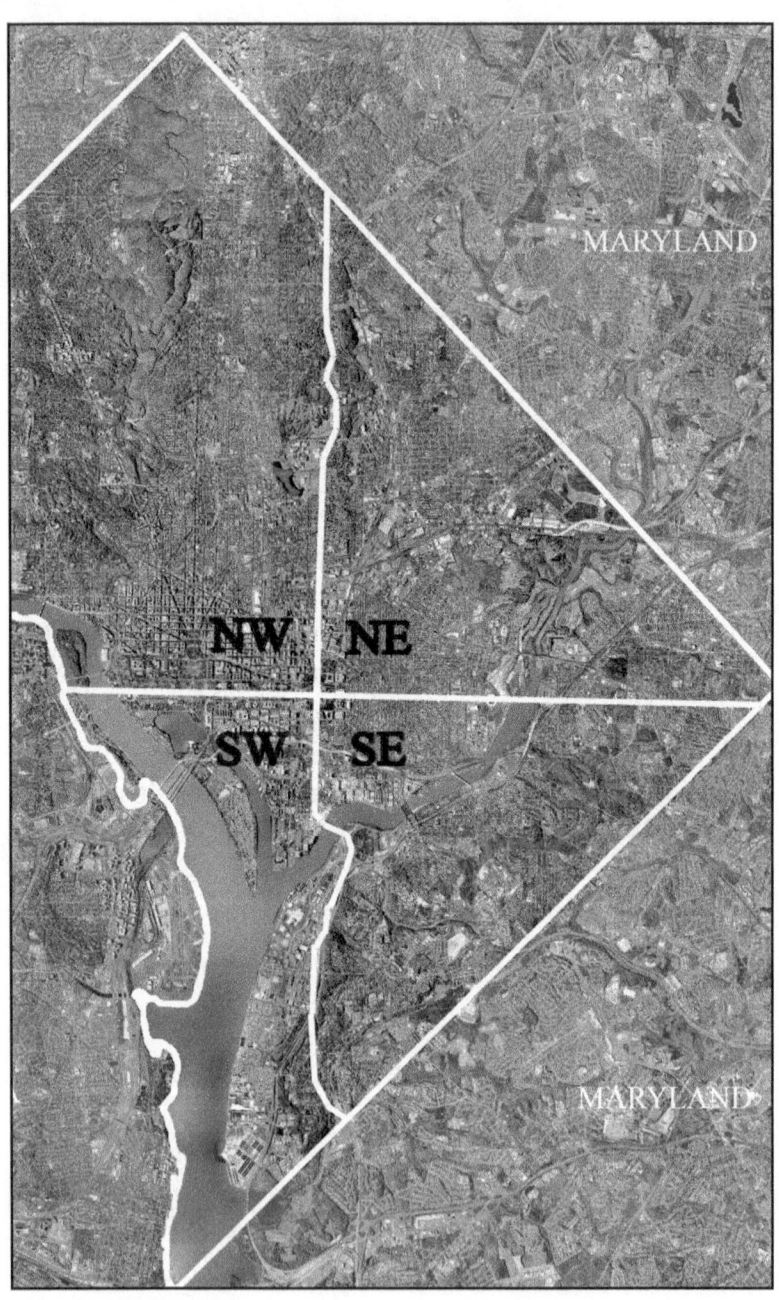

'Quadrants' of Washington, D.C. – the Capitol Building is at the center point

> *Quite simply, the cornerstone was set at that date and time because, among other things, the auspicious Caput Draconis was in Virgo...the cornerstones of the three structures that make up Federal Triangle – the Capitol, the White House, the Washington Monument – were all laid in different years but were carefully timed to occur under this exact same astrological condition.*

As mentioned above, there is only one prominent author that says L'Enfant was a Freemason – David Ovason, in his book *The Secret Architecture of Our Nation's Capital*. And the above passage from *The Lost Symbol* indicates that this book was in fact Dan Brown's source, as the Caput Draconis conjunction is one of its major themes. Ovason analyzed some twenty zodiacs found in Washington, D.C., as well as the astrological charts for important days in the construction of the capital, and discovered that construction of the capital seems to have been ruled by the veneration of the constellation Virgo:

> *The imagery of Virgo as ruler of Washington, D.C. is reflected in the considerable number of Zodiacs and lapidary symbols which grace the city. The Virgoan connection has also been emphasized in a number of foundation charts which are of fundamental importance to Washington, D.C.*[62]

Ovason echoes Langdon's "coincidence" rebuttal when he states plainly, that "whoever was directing the planning of Washington, D.C., not only had a considerable knowledge of astrology, but had a vested interest in emphasizing the role of the sign Virgo...It seems that whichever way we look in connection with the building of Washington, D.C., the beautiful Virgin always shows her face." Given this reference, it's quite surprising that Dan Brown didn't riff on this as a continuation of the wildly successful 'Sacred Feminine' meme from *The Da Vinci Code*.

In fact, Ovason and others have also raised the famous Craft image of the 'Monument to a Master Mason' as evidence that the 'sacred feminine' is a vital part of the Masonic tradition. It portrays a virgin standing above a broken column, with a sprig of acacia in her hand, and Father Time standing behind her, sometimes touching her hair. However, some have debunked this claim, with one Masonic source refuting Ovason with the following words:

> *Ovason's theory stands or falls on the assumption…that freemasons held similar views about astrology that he does, and that Freemasonry places any significance in Virgo…his assumptions are unproven and his theory fails to pass any reasonable examination.*[63]

While some Freemasons have criticized what they see as Ovason's 'mumbo-jumbo' approach in finding significance in astrological charts, others have rightly pointed out that there is a definite history of Freemasons casting horoscopes before the commencement of construction activities. For example, in their book *Talisman*, Graham Hancock and Robert Bauval confide that, after the devastation of the Great Fire of London in 1666, the early Mason Elias Ashmole was consulted about the most favorable dates for the laying of the cornerstones of important buildings.[64]

However, another area of Ovason's research regarding the geometry of Washington, D.C. is also of great interest. He points out a fascinating painting of the Washington family, by Edward Savage, which shows three members of the family discretely outlining a triangular area on a map of Washington with

Washington Family Portrait by Edward Savage

disguised hand placement.⁶⁵ Is this triangle indicating a certain location within the capital, or is it a sly 'nod of the head' to Craft members via the outline of a Masonic compass (note the looped fingers at the top of the 'triangle')? Note too that in this picture we find Washingon's grandson holding a Masonic compass above a globe, as well as a checkerboard floor – both distinctly Masonic motifs. As this painting hangs in the National Gallery of Art in Washington, D.C., it's a real shame that Dan Brown didn't have Robert Langdon dropping in to take a look, given his penchant for coded messages in paintings!

STREETS AND SYMBOLS

Many conspiracy theorists have pointed out other specific geometry which they say was also a part of the original design of the capital. Some see the Masonic square and compass design in L'Enfant's diagonal street plans (see Appendix 3) – the Capitol being the top of the compass with each leg leading to the White House and the Jefferson Memorial. Others have pointed out a 'Satanic' upside-down pentagram which can be traced to the north of the White House, with the lowest point of the symbol beginning at the Presidential residence and the Scottish Rite's House of the Temple standing at the opposite end. This is generally seen as one of the more hysterical conspiracy theories, and gets the short shrift it deserves in *The Lost Symbol*, with Robert Langdon dismissing it with the explanation "if you draw enough intersecting lines on a map, you're bound to find all kinds of shapes." Rather a change in attitude from his previous jaunts around Paris and Rome, it must be said!

On a slightly more orthodox note, Michael Baigent and Richard Leigh make quick mention of the street plan in their book about the history of Freemasonry, *The Temple and the Lodge*. All that they say is that the Capitol and the White House were each focal points of an "elaborate geometry governing the layout" of Washington, D.C. They also mention that the original design of L'Enfant was modified by Washington and Jefferson to produce octagonal patterns reminiscent of the insignia cross of the Knights Templar.

Authors Graham Hancock and Robert Bauval also mention the possibility of an intentional alignment along Pennsylvania Avenue, between the White House and the site of the Capitol building (Jenkins Hill), with the rising of the brightest star in the sky, Sirius. The heliacal rising of Sirius was of great importance to the ancient Egyptians, as it signified their New Year. The star was also closely associated with the great goddess of ancient Egypt, Isis – yet another tie-in to the sacred feminine. Hancock and Bauval point out that any observer looking along Pennsylvania Avenue at dawn in 1793 would have seen Sirius 'hovering' over the proposed site of the Capitol, a feature they believe could not have been missed by individuals like the astronomer Ellicott:

> *That such portentous astral symbolism could have gone unnoticed by the group of important Freemasons and astronomers who planned Washington and decided the locations of its principal structures, seems most unlikely.*[66]

In *Talisman*, Hancock and Bauval also suggest that the street-plan of Washington, D.C. deliberately incorporates the Kabbalistic 'Tree of Life' symbol (although truthfully, one could just as easily see the 'Rosy Cross' that Dan Brown uses in *The Lost Symbol*). They see the Capitol building as the 'head' of the esoteric symbol (designated as 'Kether'), with the Tree of Life unfolding to the west. They see the focal point of this design at a point within this giant shape corresponding to the Kabbalistic sephirah of 'Tipheret', and like Dan Brown it is the gigantic obelisk of the Washington Monument.[67] Whether or not this correspondence was planned, it is worth looking more closely at this monument, modeled on the impressive landmarks of ancient Egypt.

The Washington Monument

The cornerstone of the Washington Monument, an eleven ton block of Maryland marble, was formally laid by Grandmaster Benjamin B. French of the Grand Lodge of Free and Accepted Masons of the District of Columbia on Sunday July 4th, 1848. He is said to have worn George Washington's Masonic apron and sash, and held the same Mason's gavel that Washington had used when laying the cornerstone of the U.S. Capitol on September 18th, 1793.[68]

The Washington Monument

The idea of a monument to honor Washington was first conceived of and voted on by Congress in 1783, a full sixteen years before his death! It was originally proposed that "a Marble monument be erected by the United States in the Capitol, at the City of Washington, and that the family of George Washington be requested to permit his body to be to be deposited under it."[69] However, the refusal of the Washington family to move the former President's body after his death in December 1799 meant that the project was continually shelved.

Public displeasure at the failure of the government to create a lasting memorial for Washington finally resulted in the creation of the Washington National Monument Society, which set about raising the funds necessary through private sources. Congress set aside an area of land for the monument, and it was decided to build it at a point which aligned due south of the White House and due west of the Capitol – incidentally, a location that the original designer of Washington, D.C., Pierre L'Enfant, had marked out for a monument to Washington. However, unsuitable ground meant that it was shifted 100 yards to the south-east of this point, somewhat spoiling the alignment – though Dan Brown fails to acknowledge this when he mentions towards the end of *The Lost Symbol* that it is "due south" of the House of the Temple (nitpicking, I know).

The monument was originally planned as an obelisk 600 feet in height, with a flat apex surmounted by a 'blazing 5-pointed star' – a distinctly Masonic symbol. The base of the monument was planned to have a surrounding 'pantheon' of marble columns 100 feet high. However, shortly after the beginning of construction the planned height was reduced to 500 feet, and a pyramidion was substituted for the blazing star. Then, when the Society began to run short on resources, a plan was instituted whereby other states and countries could contribute blocks of marble (or other durable stones) to the project from their own soil.

This resulted in one of the more famous incidents in the history of the Washington Monument. The Vatican, led by Pope Pius IX, contributed a block of historic marble from the Temple of Concord in Rome, approximately 3 feet long, 10 inches thick and 18 inches high. However, the xenophobic and anti-Catholic 'American Party' (also popularly known as the 'Know-Nothings') took umbrage with the outside contribution, and vowed that the stone would never become a part of the Washington Monument.

On March 6th 1854 the "Pope's Stone", as it has come to be known, was stolen. A $100 reward was posted for its return, but the stone was never recovered. The most popular theory is that it was dumped into the nearby Potomac River, although another theory states that it was buried at the intersection of two streets in Washington, D.C.

The monument's construction continued to stutter forward, until in 1876 Congress decided enough was enough, appropriating two million dollars to finish the job. Concerns that the base of the monument was not large enough to support the towering obelisk above it led to a change in the building plans, removing many planned elements (including the pantheon and numerous columns). Instead, the base was increased in size (concealing the cornerstone forever), and the focus became the massive, solitary obelisk. The idea for a pyramidion was added at this stage, and to mimic the pyramid depicted in the Great Seal, it was constructed out of 13 rows of marble. Durable aluminium sheeting then covered the pyramidion, along with the inscription *The Lost Symbol* has now made famous, *Laus Deo*: "Praise God". It was lifted into place in 1884, more than a century after Congress had first proposed the monument to George Washington. (Incidentally, a point that Dan Brown didn't note is that the phrase *Laus Deo* also turns up in Scottish Rite Freemasonry; see the accompanying image of a Scottish Rite jewel as an example.)

Jewel of the Past Commander in Chief featuring the phrase 'Laus Deo'

Washington Monument during construction, ca. 1861

As an aside, I predicted many years ago that the Washington Monument would be a focal point of the sequel to *The Da Vinci Code*. For in that book, Brown inexplicably measures the length of the Grand Gallery in the Louvre as "three Washington Monuments laid end to end." Given Brown's concurrent research on multiple novels, and the attraction of using a monument with inherent Egyptian symbolism and importance to the landscape of the capital, it was an obvious choice.

Scottish Rite and the House of the Temple

Another location that features prominently in *The Lost Symbol* is the headquarters of the 'Mother Supreme Council' of 33rd Degree Masonry (Southern Jurisdiction of the Scottish Rite), which is located at 1733 16th Street NW in Washington, D.C. Modeled on the Mausoleum of Halicarnassus – one of the Seven Wonders of the Ancient World – this building, known as the 'House of the Temple', was designed in 1911 by the famous architect John Russell Pope and is covered in Egyptian symbols such as the Sphinx, the Ankh and the Uraeus.[70] David Ovason points out that the great tower which tops the House of the Temple is a replica of the truncated pyramid which famously decorates the reverse side of the Great Seal of the United States – right down to the detail of being constructed out of 13 courses of stonework[71] – just as the pyramidion atop the Washington Monument does. The building had two architects: with Pope not being a Freemason, a 32nd Degree Mason named Elliott Woods was also employed to work on the building. Woods' Masonic expertise was obviously necessary for the correct interior design of the Masonic temple. Ovason notes that Pope's original design had many more than 13 courses for the pyramid, but it is not known who made the decision to modify the plan.

The "Illuminati" pyramid atop the building is just one element among many that make it a perfect Dan Brown location. From the outside, this imposing edifice just screams 'secret society' (if that's not a complete contradiction in terms). Two sentinels guard the front entrance – huge stone sphinxes weighing 17 tons apiece, and carrying the names 'Wisdom' and 'Power' – behind which 33 Ionic columns, each 33 feet high, give the building a Classical look whilst symbolizing the number of degrees in the Scottish Rite. Entry is gained via a (suitably opulent-looking) bronze door, giving access to the stunning Atrium, the "central court of the Temple, where visitors are welcomed and given their first view of the majesty of the Temple's design and architecture." And majestic it is: paved with marble and lined by eight huge Doric columns of polished green Windsor granite. The limestone walls are decorated with bronze plaques bearing Masonic emblems. Alabaster bowls atop bronze lamps cast a soft glow upon the room.

Egyptian statues carved from marble guard the access to the Grand Staircase, while to each side we find the Executive

Chamber and the House of the Temple's library, which houses more than 250,000 volumes. Incidentally, Dan Brown was not writing fiction when he wrote about the 'pyramid illusion' in the library – you can see it for yourself if you visit the Scottish Rite website and view their images of the library.[72]

Ascending the Grand Staircase we are confronted with a bust of the 'father' of the Scottish Rite, Southern Jurisdiction, former confederate general Albert Pike. Engraved in the stone above the bust is a famous quote from Pike: "What we have done for ourselves alone dies with us: What we have done for others and the world remains and is immortal."

On the third floor we find the Temple Room – one of the prime locations in *The Lost Symbol*. Again, the opulence of the room stuns the eye. The floor is a mosaic created from tens of thousands of tiny marble cubes; the furniture is made from Russian Walnut, with brown pigskin upholster and finished with black and gold leaf. This finishing scheme matches the central Altar, which is made from black and gold marble. One hundred

Scottish Rite 'House of the Temple'

feet above the Altar is the huge polygonal skylight which figures in the final chapters of Dan Brown's novel. A black marble frieze on the wall surrounds the Temple Room, and is inscribed with the following words in bronze: "From the outer darkness of ignorance through the shadows of our earth life, winds the beautiful path of initiation unto the divine light of the holy altar."

Finished in 1915, the building was quickly regarded as a classic work. The January 1916 issue of the *London Architectural Review* praised John Russell Pope's design, noting that "this monumental composition may surely be said to have reached the high-water mark of achievement in that newer interpretation of the Classic style with which modern American architecture is closely identified." Pope also designed many other architectural masterpieces around Washington, D.C., including the Jefferson Memorial, the National Archives, and National Gallery of Art.

Right from the outset, Scottish Rite Freemasonry plays a major part in *The Lost Symbol*: before even opening the book, the cover image jumps out at the reader, with the wax seal impressed with the 'Double-Headed Eagle' emblem of Scottish Rite Freemasonry. Then, the opening pages detail an initiation being held at the 'House of the Temple'. Of all the different flavors of Freemasonry, Scottish Rite has perhaps the most modern conspiracy theories associated with it – so it might be worth a quick diversion here through some of the order's colorful history.

The motto that appears on the Scottish Rite seal, *Ordo ab Chao*, is just one of a number that accompany the double-headed eagle emblem. The conspiracy-flavored book *Rule By Secrecy*, by Jim Marrs – an acknowledged source for some of Dan Brown's recent research – has this to say about the motto:

> *The Masonic slogan Ordo ab Chao, or Order out of Chaos, generally is regarded as referring to the order's attempt to bring an order of knowledge to the chaos of the various*

human beliefs and philosophies in the world – a New World Order.

Conspiracy author Epperson explained that the slogan actually means the "'order' of Lucifer will replace the 'chaos' of God." Author Texe Marrs places his interpretation on a more mundane level, writing that Ordo ab Chao is a "Secret Doctrine of the Illuminati" based on the Hegelian concept that "crisis leads to opportunity." Marrs stated, "They work to invent chaos, to generate anger and frustration on the part of humans and thus, take advantage of peoples' desperate need for order."

Perhaps the main focus of conspiracy theories to do with the Scottish Rite though is Albert Pike, whose body is interred within the House of the Temple. The privileged resting place is a testament to Pike's contribution to the Scottish Rite, Southern Jurisdiction – he recomposed the forgotten rituals of the group, and was the presiding Sovereign Grand Commander of the group from 1859 until his death in 1891.

A lawyer and newspaper editor, Pike also authored a number of books on Freemasonry. The best known of these is *Morals and Dogma*, a book which was meant as a supplement to the rituals he designed for the Scottish Rite, Southern Jurisdiction. The content is a rambling commentary on ancient cultures and comparative religion, and the book was given to each initiate after they gained entrance to the 14th degree. It's interesting to note that one section of Pike's treatise is concerned with the similarities between the myths and iconography of the Egyptian goddess Isis, and the subsequent Marian tradition of Christianity.

Morals and Dogma has gained quite a reputation among conspiracy theorists and anti-Masons, due largely to the fraudulent writings of a Frenchman calling himself Léo Taxil (real name Gabriel Pagès). After originally writing a number of anti-Catholic tracts, Taxil subsequently turned his attention to Freemasonry, and focused particularly on Albert Pike. He fraudulently attributed to Pike the worship of Lucifer, and designated him as the 'Sovereign Pontiff of Universal Freemasonry'. Taxil claimed the existence of an ultra-secret sect of Masons named Palladium. However, in 1897 he revealed that his writings were hoaxes (we'll return to Taxil in a later chapter).

Nevertheless, there are many sections of *Morals and Dogma* which show that Pike was very interested in the occult, and his writings on the 'Luciferian philosophy' have no doubt provided plenty of fuel for anti-Masons. However, it is important to note that Pike's reverence for the Luciferian principle was not referring to the the Christian idea of 'Lucifer the devil', but instead to the Classical definition of Lucifer: 'the shining one' (for example, the ancient Romans named the morning star, Venus, as Lucifer). That is, Pike was a seeker of 'the light', another name for knowledge.

Pike also appeared to believe in a 'hierarchy of knowing', and wrote with disdain on much of Blue Masonry (the first three degrees). For instance:

> *The Blue Degrees are but the outer court or portico of the Temple. Part of the symbols are displayed there to the Initiate, but he is intentionally misled by false interpretations...their true explication is reserved for the Adepts, the Princes of Masonry...Masonry is the veritable Sphinx, buried to the head in the sands heaped round it by the ages.*

Pike's writings show that he was deeply interested in the Kabbalah and other strands of Hermetic thinking. In fact, the historian of the Scottish Rite, Southern Jurisdiction sees the 32 degrees of the order as being based upon the '32 paths of wisdom' in the Kabbalah.

Pike also sided with the anti-Catholic thinking of many of the medieval occultists and scientists:

> *Masonry is a search after Light. That search leads us directly back, as you see, to the Kabbalah. In that ancient and little understood medley of absurdity and philosophy, the Initiate will find the source of doctrines; and may in time come to understand the Hermetic philosophers, the Alchemist, all the Anti-Papal thinkers of the Middle Ages...*

Beyond these controversial philosophies however, Albert Pike is also embroiled in another, far stranger debate. In 1993, a group petitioned the Council of the District of Columbia to remove a statue of Albert Pike that sits in Judiciary Square in Washington, D.C. Their request was made on the basis that Albert Pike was one of the founders of the infamous Ku Klux Klan.

The Ku Klux Klan organization that we recognize today, replete with burning crosses, white hoods and lynch mobs, is actually the third incarnation of a group originally founded in Tennessee in 1865, after the end of the American Civil War. Confederate veterans originally created the group to achieve a number of goals: to aid Confederate widows and orphans of the war, to oppose the extension of voting rights to Blacks, and also to fight other 'impositions' on the southern states during the Reconstruction. According to John J. Robinson, author of *Born in Blood*:

> *The single All-Seeing Eye of Masonry became the Grand Cyclops. There were hand signals, secret passwords, secret handgrips and recognition signals, even a sacred oath, all adapted from Masonic experience. Some Klansmen even boasted of official connections between the Klan and Freemasonry.*

However, the group became known for its use of violence to achieve some of its goals, and in 1871 President Ulysses S. Grant signed the Klan Act, which authorized the use of force to end the terrorist actions of the Klan. This legislation heralded the end of the original Klan, although it was to rise again from the discontent brewing at the start of the 20th century.

The second incarnation of the KKK arrived during World War I, and was a far more successful affair. Many whites living in poverty were drawn to the group through the propaganda that their living conditions were caused by Blacks, Jews, Catholics and foreigners. The group claimed influence in the highest circles of government, allegedly inducting former President Warren Harding, and also almost wooing former President (and 33rd Degree Mason) Harry Truman. At its peak, the KKK boasted some four million members.

The most recent group going under the name of the Ku Klux Klan was not founded until after World War II, and is in essence an organization formed in response to the fledgling civil rights movement of that time. Though it shares commonalities with the original KKK, such as the desire for segregation of races, it

Ku Klux Klan march, Pennsylvania Avenue 1928

is in reality a very separate group. Any attempt to discredit Pike on the basis of his alleged role in the original KKK therefore is not really worthy of consideration, as we must consider that Pike's thinking was shared by most people in the southern states at that time (although that certainly does not validate their philosophy!). It's also worth noting that Pike was an early supporter of the rights of Native Americans.

But was Pike even involved with the original Ku Klux Klan? The only evidence linking him with the group are the writings of a number of pro-Confederate historians from the turn of the century. There is no direct evidence that he founded the group, and it must be remembered that these historians tended to glorify the Confederate role, including the Ku Klux Klan.

Nevertheless, there is some strange history linking Albert Pike with the first incarnation of the KKK. When the anti-Catholic 'Know-Nothings' group – responsible for the theft of the 'Pope Stone' in the Washington monument – dissolved, one of its members formed a new organization. The 'Knights of the Golden Circle' was formed by a 'Know-Nothing' from Virginia named George Bickley in 1856, although others have claimed that Albert Pike himself formed the group. Its aim was American (or more correctly, Southern) expansionism: a circle on the globe some 16 degrees in radius, and centered on Havana in Cuba, was earmarked as territory that should become part of America. This circle included Mexico, Central America and even some of South America. It is alleged that the infamous outlaw Jesse James was a member of the Knights of the Golden Circle.[73]

A curious aspect of Bickley's plan was his use of the number 32. He set up 32 local chapters of his new group, and the 'golden circle' itself was 32 degrees in diameter. The KGC army was also to be composed of two divisions of 16,000 soldiers each – 32,000 altogether. Is there a link here to General Pike? As we have already noted, the 32 normal degrees of Scottish Rite

Masonry, devised by Albert Pike, are said to have their basis in the 32 paths of wisdom in the Kabbalah.

In their book *Shadow of the Sentinel*, Bob Brewer and Warren Getler describe how the Knights of the Golden Circle amassed a fortune through various means, and how they hid this treasure in secret caches when the group had to go underground. The knowledge of the whereabouts of the treasure was hidden in a series of complex ciphers, waiting to be reclaimed by initiates when the time was right. Certainly prime fodder for a Dan Brown plot, although the fact that the KGC turned up in the movie *National Treasure 2* would likely make it too 'old hat' for him to use in a future novel.

It is alleged that the Knights of the Golden Circle eventually morphed into the original Ku Klux Klan. There is circumstantial evidence to support this: they shared many of the same goals, were both based on Confederate idealism, and 'Ku Klux' is actually derived from the Greek work *kyklos*, meaning 'circle' (literally, 'Circle Clan'). Note too that the Know-Nothings, the Knights of the Golden Circle, Pike's Scottish Rite Masonry and the Ku Klux Klan all shared a dislike of Catholicism. Many Masons were members of the second incarnation of the Ku Klux Klan, a fact which led the leaders of Freemasonry to purposefully distance themselves from an official affiliation.

The distrust of the Catholic Church by Scottish Rite Masons has continued into more recent history. In 1960, the Sovereign Grand Commander of the Scottish Rite, Southern Jurisdiction, wrote an article concerning the possible election of John F. Kennedy, a Catholic, as President. The article appeared in the February 1960 issue of *New Age*, a Scottish Rite publication:

> *Whatever bigotry is in evidence in the United States is exhibited solely by the Roman Catholic hierarchy...the dual*

> *allegiance of American Catholics is a present danger to our free institutions…among American citizens there should be no question or suspicion of allegiance to any foreign power, but in the case of the Roman Catholic citizen, his church is the guardian of his conscience and asserts that he must obey its laws and decrees even if they are in conflict with the Constitution and laws of the United States.*

The more fervent conspiracy theorists have taken this statement, in combination with the relatively large number of Masons involved in the JFK assassination investigation, to concoct the theory that Freemasonry (or better still, the Illuminati) was responsible for the former President's murder. However, we must remember that the anti-Catholic sentiments we read here were actually shared by the majority of Protestant Americans at the time.

Rose-Line of Washington?

There is an oblique relationship between the location of the House of the Temple and *The Da Vinci Code* which Dan Brown could have incorporated into *The Lost Symbol* if he desired. In *The Da Vinci Code*, Dan Brown remarked about the 'Rose-Line' and the meridian of Paris which passes through St Sulpice. Dr Steven Mizrach, an anthropologist at Florida International University and a respected researcher of the Priory of Sion mystery, points out that – like Paris – the U.S. capital once had its own meridian:

> *Apparently, DC was originally designed so that 16th Street would be its original north-south meridian – and this meridian was going to be the "zero meridian" of the United States. After Greenwich was made the international meridian, DC and*

Paris both renounced their claims. Today, DC uses Capitol Street as its N-S axis, but certain monuments, especially those in Meridian Hill Park, point to the older axis.[74]

The Scottish Rite's 'House of the Temple', with its 16th Street location, is also located on this same meridian. A book titled *The Jefferson Stone – Demarcation of the First Meridian of the United States*, by Silvio A. Bedini, tells how Thomas Jefferson was a driving force behind the effort to establish a prime meridian in America. This meridian was designated as passing through the mid-point of the White House. A plaque commemorating this abandoned proposal still stands today at the upper entrance to Meridian Hill Park, entered from 16th street, on the site of a previous marker established in 1816.[75] Given the ending of *The Lost Symbol*, and the direction given of 'due south' to the Washington Monument, one wonders if this meridian idea was originally a part of the novel, but was at some stage edited out.

THE PENTAGON

The Pentagon is worthy of a mention purely on the basis of its geometric construction. The five-sided shape of the building is a notable geometric figure, and also has the quality of neatly enclosing the 'magical' symbol of the pentagram (five-pointed star). Dan Brown showed his affinity for the 'Golden Section' within the pentagram in *The Da Vinci Code*, so it's surprising we didn't find a monologue regarding the headquarters of the U.S. military in *The Lost Symbol*. The pentagram symbol was first found in ancient Egypt, as a hieroglyph denoting 'star' (and by relation, the heavens).

It is said that the distinctive shape of the building arose from the problematic shape of the location originally proposed as the building site. However, a different location was later chosen, which raises the question of why the strange design was retained when the new site had none of the restrictions of the original. Another reason given for the shape of the building is that it maximizes work efficiency by making every office accessible within a few minutes walk...although we might ask why a high-rise with elevators could not have achieved the same result. In any case, construction of the building began in July 1941.

Graham Hancock and Robert Bauval point out in *Talisman* that President Franklin Delano Roosevelt, who took control of the planning of the building, was raised as a Master Freemason in 1911 and in 1929 became a 32nd Degree Scottish Rite Mason. He should therefore have been quite aware of one of Scottish Rite Masonry's key works, *Morals and Dogma* by Albert Pike, which associates the pentagon shape with the Masonic Blazing Star symbol.[76]

George Washington Masonic Memorial

Located in the independent city of Alexandria in Virginia, some six miles south of Washington, D.C., is the George Washington National Masonic Memorial. The idea of erecting a Masonic memorial to George Washington was formulated by several members of Alexandria–Washington Lodge No. 22, which had lost numerous historical treasures in a series of fires. The Lodge decided to construct a fire-proof building to house the remaining Washington memorabilia given to them by the Washington family.

Construction of the Memorial was financed entirely by voluntary contributions from members of the Masonic Fraternity. As such, it is considered to belong to all Freemasons in the United States, regardless of their 'branch' affiliation. The cornerstone was laid on November 1st, 1923, but construction proceeded only as funds became available. Thus, the Memorial was not dedicated until May 12th, 1932 – a moment described as "one of the most important and exciting events in the history of American Freemasonry."

Given its explicit Masonic association, the Memorial would certainly have made a suitable location for an extended plot diversion in *The Lost Symbol*; as it turned out, it was only mentioned quickly as a literal diversion. Nevertheless, it deserves to be discussed: the building is a spectacular landmark standing 333 feet in height, and is said to have been modeled on the ancient Pharos lighthouse of Alexandria in Egypt (another of the Seven Wonders of the Ancient World, in the same vein as the House of the Temple's link with the Mausoleum of Halicarnassus). Visitors enter the building via 'Memorial Hall' on the second floor, and are greeted by a massive sculpture of George Washington wearing his Masonic apron, just in case you were in any doubt about the association between Freemasonry and the greatest name in American history. The various floors of the building would have offered wonderful locations for Dan Brown if he had chosen to use any of them. The fourth floor contains historic memorabilia related to both Masonry and the nation's first President, while the library on the sixth floor holds some 20,000 books on the Craft – an excellent resource if Robert Langdon had chosen to use it to rectify some of the deficiencies in his knowledge of Masonry!

Elsewhere in the building can be found a 'replica' of the crypt beneath King Solomon's Temple, as well as a replica of the Ark of the Covenant. And on the uppermost floor of the Memorial is a reconstruction of the Throne Room of King Solomon's Temple, surrounded by an observation deck which provides a panoramic view of the metropolitan Washington D.C. area.

Writing in the *Scottish Rite Journal* (Feb. 2001), 33rd Degree Mason George D. Seghers described the mission of the George Washington Masonic National Memorial Association:

George Washington National Masonic Memorial (© J. Alison)

> *Our task today is not only to preserve the memory and legacy of George Washington but also to preserve, promote, and perpetuate the Masonic beliefs and ideals upon which this great nation was founded.*

Seghers' words echo the basic plotline of *The Lost Symbol*: that the United States was founded upon, and continues to be influenced by, the ideals of Freemasonry. Between the Masonic books and relics housed there, and the 'copies' of King Solomon's Temple which can be found on the higher floors, the George Washington Masonic Memorial certainly would have provided a worthy setting for *The Lost Symbol*.

WASHINGTON NATIONAL CATHEDRAL

Washington National Cathedral almost matches the Washington Monument in terms of the period over which it was constructed. The foundation stone was laid on September 29, 1907, in the presence of President (and Freemason) Theodore Roosevelt, using the mallet that George Washington used to lay the cornerstone of the Capitol with. The imposition of two world wars and the Great Depression delayed construction constantly, and the last finial wasn't placed until September 29, 1990 – 83 years to the day since construction began. It is the sixth largest cathedral in the world, and the fourth tallest structure in Washington, D.C. – though its elevated construction site means the *Gloria in Excelsis* Tower, at 91 m above the ground, is the highest point in Washington at 206 meters above sea level.

The cathedral was built with many intentional "flaws" – an architectural custom meant to illustrate the fact that only God can be perfect. Ironically, the built-in 'flaws' actually compensate for the visual distortions which accompany the viewing of massive architecture, and thus actually make the building look 'more perfect'.

Dan Brown did not invent the strange ornamentation  mentioned in *The Lost Symbol*: Washington National Cathedral does indeed feature a Darth Vader grotesque, as well as a stained glass window featuring a piece of Moon rock. On a more serious note, the cathedral is also the last resting place of a number of prominent American individuals, including Hellen Keller and President Woodrow Wilson.

The Capitol and the Apotheosis of Washington

The United States Capitol building has always been the centerpiece of Washington, D.C., right back to L'Enfant's original plans. The French-born architect placed "Congress House" – soon to be renamed the Capitol on the insistence of Thomas Jefferson – on Jenkin's Hill, the highest point in his city plan. Replaced in 1792 after a disagreement with George Washington, L'Enfant however never got to bring his plans to life, though his planned location was retained as the site of this majestic building.

A competition was announced by Thomas Jefferson in 1792 to try and fill L'Enfant's shoes. The winning entry was a design by architect William Thornton, drawing inspiration from the Louvre in Paris and the Pantheon in Rome. However, several modifications were subsequently made, perhaps most notably by Freemason Benjamin Latrobe.

As previously mentioned, the cornerstone of the Capitol was laid by George Washington on September 18, 1793. Descending into the trench wearing his Masonic apron, Washington deposited a silver plate, and then laid upon it the cornerstone of the Capitol, followed by the standard Masonic 'offerings' of corn, wine and oil. The following words were inscribed upon the silver plate:

> This South East Corner Stone, of the Capitol of the United States of America in the City of Washington, was laid on the 18th day of September, 1793, in the Thirteenth year of American Independence, in the first year of the second term of the Presidency of George Washington, whose virtues in the civil administration of his country have been as conspicuous and beneficial, as his Military valour and prudence have been useful in establishing her liberties, and in the year of Masonry 5793, by the President of the United States, in concert with the Grand Lodge of Maryland, several Lodges under its jurisdiction, and Lodge No. 22, from Alexandria, Virginia.

Thornton's original plans, inspired by the Pantheon, included a dome, but one was not built until 1823 under the orders of

Capitol dome under construction during inauguration of President Lincoln

the third Architect of the Capitol, Charles Bulfinch. However, as extensions were built onto the north and south wings of the Capitol in order to house the growing size of the U.S. Congress, Bulfinch's original dome became an eyesore.

In 1855, legislation was passed to build a bigger dome. The new dome was designed by Thomas U. Walter, the fourth Architect of the Capitol. Costing more than a million dollars, construction took place between 1855 and 1866. The new dome was built from more than 4000 metric tons of iron, and stood 88 meters tall with the statue of Freedom included. Inside the view is stunning – the ceiling rises to 55 meters above the Rotunda floor, and looking up through the oculus of the dome one is greeted with the exquisite sight of Constantino Brumidi's fresco *The Apotheosis of Washington*.

When we take a closer look at Brumidi's fresco some fascinating elements grab our attention. The painting, taking up more than 4000 square feet in area, features not only the ascended George Washington (*à la* the earlier apotheosis depictions mentioned in the previous chapter), but also various other figures. In the center of the image, Washington is flanked by the goddesses Liberty and Victory, along with 13 maidens representing the original 13 colonies. Outside of this group there are six scenes painted representing various aspects of the nation: War, Science, Marine, Commerce, Mechanics, and Agriculture. Perhaps the most interesting is the depiction of Science: Minerva, the Roman goddess of crafts and wisdom stands amongst a group of great American scientists, including Benjamin Franklin, Samuel Morse and Robert Fulton. To the left of the main group, an individual is using a compass or pair of dividers – a possible reference to Freemasonry? Notably, Franklin and Fulton were both Masons.

Directly beneath the rotunda lies the United States Capitol Crypt, a large circular room filled with forty neoclassical Doric

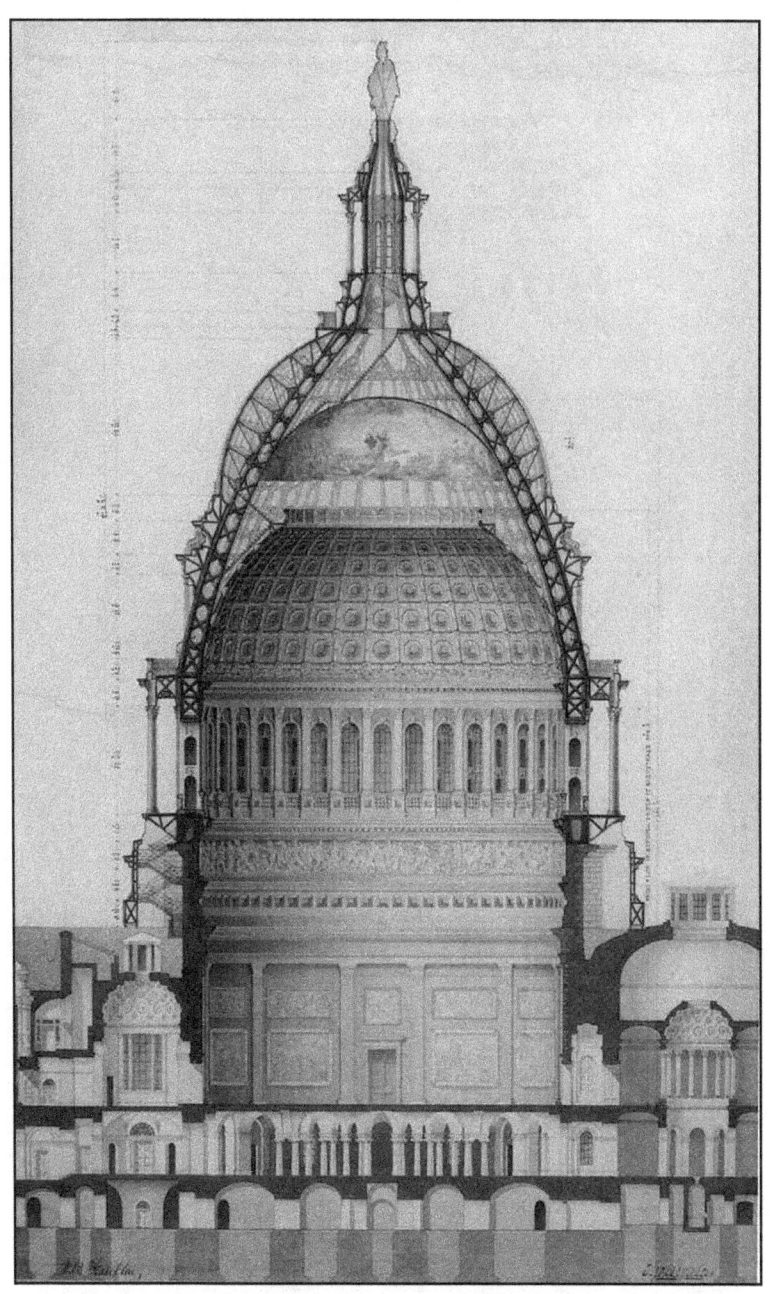

Plan of the U.S. Capitol dome

Funeral of President Gerald Ford in United States Capitol Rotunda

columns. Originally designed as an entrance to Washington's Tomb (before his family refused to have his body moved there), it now instead houses a museum and gift shop. A marble compass is embedded in the floor of the Crypt, marking the center point of the District of Columbia from which the four quadrants of Washington, D.C. originate.

Kryptos

As readers of *The Lost Symbol* now know, located in the courtyard and surroundings of C.I.A. headquarters in Langley is a sculpture named "Kryptos". Created by American artist James Sanborn, Kryptos is actually a number of sculptures, although the most recognized piece is a large vertical "S" shaped copper screen inscribed with 865 characters, in which four separate messages are encoded, each with its own cipher. Sanborn has revealed that there is an additional riddle which will be solvable only after the four encrypted passages have been decrypted. Since its dedication in 1990, three of the four codes have been cracked, while the fourth remains unsolved.

Apparently Dan Brown, a self-confessed cryptography nut, has long been interested in the Kryptos story. In fact, some early rumors suggested that he was working closely with Sanborn as part of *The Lost Symbol*. It's interesting to note that some reports on Kryptos do say that Sanborn "collaborated with a prominent fiction writer in composing the text to be encoded," but Sanborn himself has since said that while he considered the idea when beginning the sculpture, "I decided not to do it, why let someone else in on the secret?" However, it's also worth pointing out that Kryptos was created well before Dan Brown's time as a fiction writer (it was dedicated in 1990), and in an interview with *Wired Magazine* prior to the publication of *The Lost Symbol*, Sanborn was said to be "deeply annoyed" at the prospect of Kryptos being used as a plot device in the new novel.

The solutions to the first three sections are:

Solution 1: "Between subtle shading and the absence of light lies the nuance of Iqlusion [sic]"

Solution 2: "It was totally invisible hows that possible? They used the Earth's magnetic field. The information was gathered and transmitted undergruund [sic] to an unknown location. Does Langley know about this? They should its buried out there somewhere. Who knows the exact location? Only WW this was his last message. Thirty eight degrees fifty seven minutes six point five seconds north seventy seven degrees eight minutes forty four seconds west. Layer two.

Solution 3: Slowly desparatly [sic] slowly the remains of passage debris that encumbered the lower part of the doorway was removed with trembling hands I made a tiny breach in the upper left hand corner and then widening the hole a little I

Main Kryptos sculpture at C.I.A. headquarters, Langley

inserted the candle and peered in the hot air escaping from the chamber caused the flame to flicker but presently details of the room within emerged from the mist. Can you see anything?

In a TV interview conducted long before *The Lost Symbol* was published, Dan Brown – when asked about the sculpture – replied that it "refers to the ancient mysteries." Brown's opinion no doubt comes from the third solution, which is a paraphrase from Howard Carter's account of the opening of the tomb of Tutankhamun in his 1923 book *The Tomb of Tutankhamun*. Not to mention that Mal'akh's thought about the lost pyramid – "it is buried out there somewhere" – is a direct quote from the second Kryptos passage.

Most people have assumed that the 'WW' referred to in the second solution is the C.I.A. director at the time of the sculpture's dedication, William Webster. The C.I.A., no doubt wary of an embarrassing message being encoded by the artist, had insisted that Sanborn give Webster an envelope containing the code and the message. Thus, WW should certainly know the solution. Others have cautioned against such an easy answer, and continue to search for other options – some people have even pointed out that WW turned upside down is MM, the initials of Mary Magdalene, a name that featured in *The Da Vinci Code*. However, James Sanborn has said categorically that this is not the solution, and (if we can take his word) has confirmed that WW does in fact reference Webster.

An Endless List of Possibilities

There are numerous other locations in Washington, D.C. which Dan Brown could easily have inserted into the plot of *The Lost Symbol* – really, in setting the novel in the United States capital he was spoilt for choice when it comes to esoteric landmarks (which makes the selection of the Botanica Gardens somewhat of a curiosity). For example, there are a curious number of areas in the capital named after Egyptian place names, such as Alexandria. Even better though, Washington, D.C. also has a neighbourhood and Metro stop named Rosslyn! Given the ending of *The Da Vinci Code* at the enigmatic Rosslyn Chapel in Scotland, and the proximity of this namesake to the National Mall (it sits just across the Potomac), it is a wonder that it wasn't mentioned in *The Lost Symbol*, if even briefly. There are also various 'coincidences' which could have been called on as being of historical interest: for example, the White House cornerstone ceremony was held on October 13th, the Templars' day of infamy.

Naturally enough, the United States capital is filled with monuments – some of which are well-known, some of which are less well-known but display esoteric symbolism. For instance, the headquarters of the Internal Revenue Service (I.R.S.) has some distinctive sculptures surrounding it such as a small pyramid at its entrance, as well as a hand pointing a finger to the heavens – a gesture which receives plenty of attention in Picknett and Prince's book *The Templar Revelation* as an 'insignia' of Leonardo Da Vinci, and which Dan Brown included in *The Da Vinci Code*.

Let's finish with a quick run-down of some of the more obscure locations which could have figured in *The Lost Symbol*, due to their similarity with settings in the previous Robert Langdon books:

- The Department of Commerce building, in which David Ovason correlates the Mining, Fisheries, Commerce and Aeronautics tympana with the elements Earth, Water, Fire and Air – a central theme of *Angels and Demons*.

- A memorial statue to assassinated President James Garfield near the Capitol building which features Masonic symbolism.

- A marble sculpture within the Capitol building named *The Car of History*, carved by Carlo Franzoni in 1819, which features a goddess in a chariot surrounded by astrological symbolism.

- *Freedom*, the 20-foot-high statue of a goddess which surmounts the dome of the Capitol building, sculpted by Freemason Thomas Crawford.

- The statue of Scottish Rite patriarch, and Confederate general Albert Pike, which stands at 3rd and D Streets NW. As mentioned above, Pike's statue has recently been at the centre of a controversy with suggestions that he was a founder of the Ku Klux Klan.

If you'd like more detailed information on the esoteric architecture of Washington, D.C., take a look at David Ovason's book and also Christopher Hodapp's more recent *Solomon's Builders*, which is written from the point of view of a Freemason (and with Dan Brown's novel in mind). At this point though, we'll leave this subject and begin delving into Masonic conspiracy theories, and the strange symbolism on the Great Seal of the United States.

CHAPTER 5

A MASONIC CONSPIRACY?

The Great Seal of the United States has probably been the subject of more conspiracy theories than any other national symbol. The two-sided seal depicts an eagle on its 'front', holding both arrows and olive branches. On the reverse side we find the more controversial image, a truncated pyramid with an 'All-Seeing Eye' as its pyramidion – a symbol that many have associated with a conspiracy headed by the group called 'the Illuminati'.

Each time the Great Seal is mentioned in *The Lost Symbol*, Dan Brown generally does so with a dismissal of ideas promulgated by "conspiracy theorists". However, it's interesting to note that the Great Seal made a brief appearance in *Angels and Demons*, the first Robert Langdon book, and at that time Robert Langdon viewed it as an Illuminati symbol which had been put on the dollar bill by Freemasons! Additionally, when asked what he thought these symbols had to do with the United States in an interview a number of years ago, Brown answered...

> *...absolutely nothing, which is what makes their presence on our currency so remarkable...the eye inside the triangle is a pagan symbol adopted by the Illuminati to signify the brotherhood's ability to infiltrate and watch all things.*

It seems that both Dan Brown and Robert Langdon's views on the conspiratorial themes of the Great Seal have changed somewhat over the past decade!

Another book by the author David Ovason might be worth consulting on this topic. *The Secret Symbols of the Dollar Bill* provides comprehensive information about the symbolism of the Seal and its later incorporation into the United States dollar bill. The esoteric author Manly Hall also discusses the Great Seal in some of his work, so we'll see what he has to say as well. Lastly, we'll finish off with a look at the possibility that the emblem encapsulates the idea of Francis Bacon's 'New Atlantis', and that it may still be a goal of some of those in power today – more than two hundred years after the Declaration of Independence.

History of the Great Seal

Before adjourning on the ground-breaking day of July 4, 1776, the Continental Congress passed a resolution that a committee be formed to design a seal for the newly independent United States. The members chosen were Benjamin Franklin, John Adams and Thomas Jefferson – three of the five men who worked on the Declaration of Independence, two of whom would go on to become President. However, it would take another six years before the Great Seal of the United States came into being, with two more committees and fourteen men eventually employed to establish the icon.

The first committee of Franklin, Adams and Jefferson initially worked on Biblical and classical themes, including the 'Children of Israel in the Wilderness',[77] but with little success. They then employed the talents of French portrait artist, Pierre Eugene du Simitiere, who had some experience in designing seals. However, the du Simitiere-influenced design was rejected by Congress on August 20th 1776, although a couple of the features later became a part of the official seal – the infamous Eye of Providence within a triangle, and the motto *E Pluribus Unum*.[78]

Four years later, a second committee was appointed to take over the design of the Great Seal. They asked Francis Hopkinson, who had contributed to the design of both the American flag and the great seal of the State of New Jersey, to serve as consultant on the project. However, Congress rejected this design as well. Like the previous effort though, some features were retained in later designs – the 13 red and white stripes on the shield held by the eagle, the constellation of 13 six-pointed stars, and the olive branch as a symbol of peace.[79]

In May 1782, Congress appointed a third committee to continue with the design. This they did with maximum efficiency – by promptly assigning the job to a lawyer from Philadelphia named William Barton. Barton added the important figure of the eagle to the design, and also designed the enigmatic pyramid found on the reverse of the seal, combining it with the first committee's Eye of Providence. Barton worked quickly, and the third committee turned in its report to Congress just five days after being appointed.

However, the ever-fussy Congress was still not satisfied, and the project became the responsibility of Charles Thomson, Secretary of Congress. Though not a great artist, Thomson was able to incorporate the various features into an acceptable design, while also adding the Latin mottoes *Annuit Coeptis* and *Novus Ordo Seclorum* to the reverse of the seal. He then employed Barton again to finish the job artistically, and finally the Great Seal of the United States was accepted by Congress on June 20th 1782.

The Obverse of the Seal

The obverse side of the Great Seal today depicts a Bald Eagle with outstretched wings. In its left claw it holds a bundle of arrows, while in the right we find an olive branch – the head of the eagle is turned to its right, which is said to indicate that the United States favors peace, although it is always prepared to make war if necessary. Though the United States does not have an official coat-of-arms, the eagle image is often used in its place.

Manly Hall, in *The Secret Teachings of All Ages*, claims that the bird portrayed on the original seal was not in fact an eagle, but the mythological phoenix. He based this claim on the small tuft of feathers rising from the back of its head, similar to Egyptian depictions of the Phoenix. Hall says:

> *In the Mysteries it was customary to refer to initiates as 'phoenixes' or 'men who had been born again'...born into a consciousness of the spiritual world.*[80]

According to Manly Hall, the "hand of the Mysteries" was involved in the founding of the United States, and the Great Seal acts as its signature. He does admit though that only a student of symbolism is fit to see through the subterfuge of the modern-day claim that the bird is an eagle. Hall is at the very least partly correct with his claim, because one of the early designs – by William Barton – clearly shows a phoenix sitting upon its characteristic nest of flames. We'll continue to call it an eagle, for the sake of simplicity, but Hall's claims are worth keeping in mind.

The eagle holds in its beak a banner which reads *E Pluribus Unum*, meaning 'Out of many, One'. This is a reference to the joining of the original thirteen colonies into the United States of America – fittingly, there are thirteen letters in the phrase itself. But this is probably more than a coincidence, for the number thirteen is in fact found throughout the Great Seal: there are thirteen arrows in the eagle's left claw, the shield is made up of thirteen stripes, and above the eagle there are thirteen stars. Remember too that the pyramid at the top of the House of the Temple and the pyramidion atop the Washinton Monument are both constructed with thirteen courses, and Washington is accompanied by thirteen maidens in Brumidi's *Apotheosis of Washington*. It perhaps should be noted then, that thirteen is also a 'power number' in Freemasonry.

One point noted by conspiracy theorists is that the thirteen stars above the head of the eagle are arranged to form the 'Seal of Solomon', a hexagram also known as the 'Star of David'. This often leads to fanciful accusations of a Jewish conspiracy, although some researchers have suggested that the financier Haym Solomon may have been involved in the placement of this 'constellation'. Interestingly, the individual stars in the

Obverse of the Great Seal

hexagram design were originally hexagrams themselves, but were changed into pentagrams at some point.[81]

We have already noted the symbolism of the pentagram, but there is one additional side-note worthy of mention. In *The Secret Symbols of the Dollar Bill,* David Ovason raises the possibility that the earliest official use of the five-pointed star in North America may have been at the request of none other than Francis Bacon.[82]

The Reverse of the Seal

If the obverse of the Great Seal raises some eyebrows, the reverse side is a veritable feast for the conspiracy theorist. The primary motif on the back side of the seal is an unfinished pyramid consisting of thirteen courses of masonry. Some say the image is very similar to the pyramids of Central America. It is more likely though, that it is a simplistic illustration of the Great Pyramid of Giza, in Egypt. This wonder of the ancient world, which stands some 450 feet in height, is also missing its capstone. It consists of substantially more than thirteen courses of masonry though!

At the base of the pyramid the year 1776 is inscribed in Roman numerals. This is said to refer to the date of the Declaration of Independence of the United States. However, to conspiracy theorists the date has a second meaning, for on May 1st 1776 Adam Weishaupt formed the Order of the Bavarian Illuminati. This is just one piece of evidence that is said to point to the seal being an emblem of the Illuminati brotherhood.

Above the truncated pyramid hovers the so-called 'Eye of Providence', contained within a triangle. Brown says this particular feature is "symbolic of the Illuminati's desire to bring about 'enlightened change' from the myth of religion to the truth of science." However, others – funnily enough, Masons included – have said the combination of pyramid and all-seeing eye was not a motif of Freemasonry at the time, and that the association probably arose in 1884 when Harvard professor, Eliot Norton, wrote that the emblem was...

> ...*practically incapable of effective treatment; it can hardly, (however artistically treated by the designer), look otherwise than as a dull emblem of a Masonic fraternity.*[83]

The claim that Norton provided the Masonic context of the Great Seal design is certainly mistaken, if not disingenuous. David Ovason points out numerous rebuttals – one of the earliest uses of the all-seeing eye was by Freemason and founder of the Royal Society, Robert Moray.[84] The personal seal of Moray, which can be found on his private correspondence, has a radiant eye at its center – and incidentally also features a five-pointed star. The pyramid was a common image in early 18th century lodges, and a Lodge Summons dated 1757, to the Philadelphia Ancient Lodge No. 2 clearly portrays the all-seeing eye.

Moreover, there are more direct links between the 'all-seeing eye' and the Founding Fathers. As Ovason points out in *The Secret Architecture of Our Nation's Capital*, Benjamin Franklin would almost certainly have been conversant with the work of the French Freemason Theodore Tschoudy, who equated French Freemasonry with a blazing five-pointed star carrying within it the all-seeing eye.[85] And if anybody still has any doubt that the Founding Fathers were 'in' on the Masonic symbolism of the all-seeing eye, I would gently direct them to look at the Masonic apron of Brother George Washington on the following page.

Two mottoes appear on the reverse side of the seal. Across the top of the Great Seal we see the Latin phrase *Annuit*

Masonic apron of George Washington

Coeptis, which is generally translated as 'He has favored our undertaking'. Around the bottom a separate phrase is inscribed, *Novus Ordo Seclorum*, taken to mean 'a new order of the ages'. Note that two of the three mottoes on the Great Seal are made up of thirteen letters. Beyond that fact though, there is also an eye-opening geometrical code to be found in the two mottoes written on the reverse of the Great Seal, although it is not known whether it was put there on purpose or was simply a bizarre coincidence. Dan Brown found it interesting enough to include it in *The Lost Symbol* though.

Those with sharp eyes have found that a hexagram, or 'Seal of Solomon', can be constructed overlaying this side of the seal. If one circles the 'A' in 'Annuit', the 's' in 'Coeptis', the 'N' in 'Novus', the final 'o' in 'Ordo' and the 'm' in 'Seclorum', we have five quite equidistant points, apart from one large gap. It is quite obvious that making another circle at the top of the 'All-seeing eye' triangle will give six points from which a hexagram can be constructed. While the ability to fit a hexagram so neatly on the seal is interesting enough, the real excitement comes when we look at the letters we circled to do so – A, S, N, O and M. Anyone with a degree of skill in constructing anagrams will see that there is one very relevant possibility from this set of letters – the word MASON. The question is: was it intentional? It might be worth noting that various people involved in the creation of the Great Seal – including chairman of the second panel, James Lovell, and Thomas Jefferson – were skilled cryptographers. Of course, this isn't evidence that the MASON anagram was intentional though…and Dan Brown seems to think that it's all much ado about nothing.

One last point while we are discussing the Latin mottoes: we should also note that there is some confusion on the meaning of the Latin word *seclorum* – the orthodox opinion is that the word originated with the classical poet Virgil, in which context it meant 'for all time', or 'for the ages'. However, others – including Dan Brown – have tied the word to the modern 'secular', and its opposition to 'religious'. In Brown's own words, *Novus Ordo Seclorum* is a "clear call to the secular or non-religious." This theme ties in well with the Rosicrucian tradition running through Francis Bacon and the subsequent 'Royal Society', right up to Benjamin Franklin, Thomas Jefferson and Thomas Paine – who were all scientists and Deists. The question is: has this tradition survived into modern times?

Anti-Christ Superstar

Any secret society, by its very nature, is bound to be the subject of rumor and accusations. Add to that any whiff of magical or hermetic thinking and those of the 'orthodox' point of view are sure to feel threatened. Masonry is no different: as early as 1698, almost two decades before the 'official' beginnings of Freemasonry, we find pamphlets warning of the danger of the Craft:

> *For this devilish sect are Meeters in secret which swere against all without their Following. They are the Anti-Christ which was to come leading them from Fear of God. For how should they meet in secret places and with secret Signs taking care that none observe them to do the Work of God; are not these the Ways of Evil-dom?* [86]

The Papal Bulls condemning Freemasonry in the mid-18th century would only have served to fuel the conspiratorial fires in the public consciousness. Then, at the end of the 18th century, the 'overthrow' of the British in the American colonies and the monarchy in France – at least partly under the influence of known Masons – would have created an inferno. In some quarters, the execution of the King of France was seen as a revenge killing by the Templars on behalf of their last master, Jacques de Molay.

A number of books appeared immediately after the French Revolution began, accusing Freemasons of masterminding the action. Then, in 1797, came arguably the most influential 'anti-Masonry' book of the past two centuries: *Mémoires pour servir à l'histoire du jacobinisme*, by Abbe Augustin de Barruel. Educated by the Jesuits, Barruel claimed to have been initiated as a Master Mason, but did not make a vow of secrecy and thus felt he could warn the public of the alleged dangers of the Craft. On the other hand, some might be tempted to see the hand of the Jesuit order in this book's attack on Freemasonry.

At the same time in Scotland, a Professor of Natural Philosophy at the University of Edinburgh began his own book on the 'Masonic conspiracy'. John Robison had been initiated as a Mason in the early 1770s, but had lost interest soon after and discontinued his membership. However, the events of the following two decades led him to re-examine the aspirations of his former brethren, and as a result he published a book titled *Proofs of a Conspiracy against all the Religions and Governments of Europe, Carried on in the Secret Meetings of Freemasons, Illuminati, and Reading Societies*. Much of the material used today by conspiracy theorists derives from the works of Barruel and Robison, even though the majority of the content of these books appears to be no more than innuendo and rumor.

The threat of an Illuminati conspiracy was present in the minds of many people around the world, and even George Washington was appraised of this alleged conspiracy. In reply to a letter he had received regarding Robison's book, Washington defended Freemasonry – although he also appears to have mispresented his own involvement with Masonic lodges:

> *I have heard much of the nefarious, and dangerous plan, and doctrines of the Illuminati, but never saw the Book until you were pleased to send it to me…The fact is, I preside over [no English Lodges], nor have I been in one more than once or twice, within the last thirty years. I believe notwithstanding, that none of the Lodges in this Country are contaminated with the principles ascribed to the Society of the Illuminati.*

In a second letter, Washington continues to talk about the reputation of the Illuminati:

> *It was not my intention to doubt that, the Doctrines of the Illuminati, and principles of Jacobinism had not spread in the United States. On the contrary, no one is more truly satisfied of this fact than I am.*

> *The idea that I meant to convey, was, that I did not believe that the Lodges of Free Masons in this Country had, as Societies, endeavoured to propagate the diabolical tenets of the first, or pernicious principles of the latter (if they are susceptible of seperation). That Individuals of them may have done it, or that the founder, or instrument employed to found, the Democratic Societies in the United States, may have had these objects; and actually had a seperation of the People from their Government in view, is too evident to be questioned.*

Washington's letters are a graphic illustration of the conspiratorial fever that Barruel and Robison's books had engendered. Fearful monarchies across Europe clamped down on secret societies and fraternities to minimize the possibility of being the 'next France'. Meanwhile, in the United States, a great controversy would erupt within three decades which would change the face of Freemasonry.

In 1826, a man by the name of William Morgan came into dispute with Masonic lodges in the New York area. As revenge, he began work on an exposé of the Craft, which caused mayhem in the local Freemasonry community. On 10 September 1826, shortly after he had received the copyright for his book, *Illustrations of Masonry*, the publisher's print shop was set ablaze. The next day, Morgan was arrested on charges of petty theft. Subsequently released due to a lack of evidence, Morgan was immediately rearrested on debt charges and imprisoned. A day later, Morgan was abducted from his jail cell in the dark of night, and was never seen again.

Some say Morgan was murdered, while others suggest he was 'resettled' in Canada. Whatever the fate of William Morgan, the impact on Freemasonry was huge. The trumped up charges, abduction of a man from a jail cell, the superficial investigation of the crime and subsequent light penalties imposed on Morgan's abductors suggested a conspiracy. Given Morgan's threats to Freemasonry, and the fact as many as two-thirds of office-holders across New York State belonged to Masonic lodges, many people felt that Freemasonry had overstepped its bounds, and was now controlling government, the judicial system, and law enforcement. In the wake of the Morgan affair, an anti-Masonic social movement began in New York, and quickly spread to other states. Freemasonry was condemned as being anti-Christian and anti-democratic. It's also interesting to note the position that women took: they joined the movement in significant numbers, perhaps alienated by the male-only membership restriction, and perhaps by the idea that their husbands were being made to keep secrets from them.

The movement quickly grew in influence, and just a year after Morgan's disappearance it became the first 'third party' in American politics. In 1832 the 'Anti-Masonic Party' ran their own candidate, William Wirt, for president of the United States, against Andrew Jackson and Henry Clay – both of whom were Freemasons. However, Wirt only carried the state of Vermont, and the poor showing for the party led to its rapid demise on the national political scene. It eventually disbanded in 1843.

The disappearance of William Morgan, and subsequent rise in anti-Masonry feeling, led to a rapid decline in Masonic membership and visibility. It would take more than two decades for the Craft to recover from the debacle.

Freemasonry would never fully rid itself of the aura of conspiracy however. At the end of the 19th century a notorious hoax was perpetrated by one Leo Taxil (a pen name of Gabriel Jogand-Pagès). After publishing anti-clerical material (including an 'exposé' of the love life of Pope Pius IX) during the early 1880s, Taxil suddenly became the darling of the Catholic Church when he began writing books attacking Freemasonry. Taxil told of secret rituals in which Lucifer was worshipped, women's lodges being used as Masonic brothels, and a Masonic cabal known as Palladium intent on world domination. Taxil's publications, in association with an accomplice writing under the name of 'Doctor Bataille', became famous across the world, even though, as Jay Kinney says in his excellent book *The Masonic Myth*, the pair went "so far into the realm of the unbelievable that his avid Catholic readers should have been tipped off to the existence of a hoax." For example Bataille tells of a magical telephonic system used by the leaders of Palladium named the Arcula Mystica (the Mystic Box):

> *When the Supreme Dogmatical chief wishes to communicate, for example, with the head of political action, he presses his finger on the Statuette Ignis and on the Statuette Ratio: these sink into their sockets and at the same instant, a strong whistling is heard in Rome, in the office where Lemmi keeps his Arcula Mystica; Lemmi opens his box and sees the statuette of Ignis sunk, while tiny, harmless flames issue from the throat of the silver toad. Then he knows that the Soverign Pontiff of Charlestson wishes to speak to him.*

Taxil was eventually outed as the fraudster that he was, and in 1897 he confessed publicly that the entire story was a hoax. This hasn't stopped his books from becoming a major source of anti-Masonic literature over the past century however.

New World Order in Your Pocket

If the Morgan affair came to dominate Masonic conspiracy thinking in the 19th century, then the 20th century can boast its own defining moment. Curiously enough, it features the re-emergence of the esoteric figures on the Great Seal. In 1934 the United States Secretary of Agriculture, Henry Wallace, became interested in the mysterious iconography of the seal. There is a good reason for this, as Wallace was a mystically oriented Freemason initiated to the 32nd Degree in the Scottish Rite, affiliated with the District of Columbia Scottish Rite body.[87]

Wallace decided to show the seal to President Franklin Roosevelt. Wallace described the meeting:

> *Roosevelt...was first struck with the representation of the all-seeing eye – a Masonic representation of the Great Architect of the Universe. Next, he was impressed with*

the idea that the foundation for the new order of the ages had been laid in 1776 but that it would be completed only under the eye of the Great Architect. Roosevelt, like myself, was a 32nd Degree Mason. He suggested that the Seal be put on the dollar bill.[88]

Though the Secretary of the Treasury at the time, Henry Morgenthau, was also a Freemason, he apparently was not happy with the inclusion of the esoteric symbolism. "It was not till later that I learned that the pyramid...had some cabalistic significance for members of a small religious sect," Morgenthau later wrote.[89] Since that time though, this controversial move has been at the center of Masonic conspiracy allegations. Henry Wallace went on to become Vice-President of the United States. Roosevelt, the 32nd President and a 32nd degree Mason, was succeeded by Harry Truman, the 33rd President and a 33rd degree Freemason.[90]

Wallace was a fascinating character: he was raised in Des Moines, Iowa, as a Presbyterian, but throughout his life went on to explore astrology, reincarnation, Freemasonry, Eastern religions, Native American mysticism, Theosophy and occultism. In his own words, Wallace was "a searcher for methods of bringing the 'inner light' to outward manifestation and raising outward

Unfinished Pyramid on the Dollar Bill

manifestation to the inner light." He was also, in the opinion of historian Arthur Schlesinger, Jr., "the best secretary of agriculture the country has ever had."[91]

Wallace also spoke of the familiar concept of a 'New World Order', a subject sure to raise alarm bells with conspiracy theorists. Lynn Picknett and Clive Prince – authors of Dan Brown favourite *The Templar Revelation* – point out in their book *The Stargate Conspiracy* that Wallace said in 1934:

> *It will take a more definite recognition of the Grand Architect of the Universe before the apex stone is finally fitted into place and this nation in the full strength of its power is in position to assume leadership among the nations in inaugurating 'the new order of the ages'.*[92]

Around the same time that Wallace made this statement, the famous psychic healer Edward Cayce had this to say in one of his 'readings':

> *Americanism with the universal thought that is expressed and manifest in the Brotherhood of man into group thought, as expressed by the Masonic order, will be the eventual rule in the settlement of affairs in the world.*[93]

In a government-commissioned report of 1973, Freemasonry is recommended as a tonic to the diverse changes occurring in American society. The author of the report, Willis Harman, later wrote about the Great Seal:

> *The specific symbols associated with the nation's birth have an additional significance. It is under these symbols, principle and goals, properly understood, and no others, that the differing viewpoints within the nation can be ultimately reconciled.*[94]

Needless to say, conspiracy theorists and religious fundamentalists get a little hysterical about the Great Seal. Television evangelist Pat Robertson claimed in his 1991 book *The New World Order* that the emblem was a primary piece of evidence of a conspiracy by Freemasonry to create an anti-Christian global government, a "world order under a mystery religion designed to replace the old Christian world order of Europe and America." One can only wonder what Robertson thinks of *The Lost Symbol*!

Henry Wallace's statements regarding the capstone being 'fitted into place' were to have a peculiar epilogue at the turn of the millennium. After a golden capstone was ceremoniously placed on the Egyptian obelisk which stands at the Place de la Concorde in Paris in May 1998, the Egyptian Minister of Culture announced that a similar ceremony would take place at the Great Pyramid of Giza at midnight on New Year's Eve 1999. The Egyptian government announced the gala event would feature a musical performance by Jean-Michael Jarre – with a theme revolving around the astrological zodiac – during which the 'Eye of Horus' was to be projected upon the pyramids. Then, at midnight, the event would culminate with a helicopter placing a gold capstone on the Great Pyramid, to symbolically complete it. Thus, the first light of the 'New Age' would strike the capstone before anything else in this sacred location, in a similar manner to Dan Brown's discussion of the capstone of the Washington Monument in *The Lost Symbol*.

This idea was a highly charged one – placing the capstone on the Great Pyramid would have suggested, in a symbolic sense, that humanity had become perfected. Just as there are flaws built into Washington National Cathedral to show that only God is perfect, so too do esoteric texts – such as Manly Hall's *Secret Teachings of All Ages* – say that the Great Pyramid was left unfinished due to "a curious tendency among the builders of great religious edifices to leave their creations unfinished, thereby signifying that God alone is complete." In Hall's words, "as a rough and unfinished block, man is taken from the quarry and by the secret culture of the Mysteries gradually transformed into a trued and perfect pyramidal capstone. The temple is complete only when the initiate himself becomes the living apex through which the divine power is focused into the diverging structure below."

In his 1996 book *Temple of the Cosmos*, Jeremy Naydler elaborates on one particular story about the significance of the capstone being replaced on the pyramid. It could well be the source for the myth recounted in *The Lost Symbol* about a "buried pyramid", as it shares a number of elements:

> Originally the Great Pyramid of Khufu had its capstone in place. It was gold-plated, and on each of its four sides a blue eye of Horus was painted. When the sun struck the pyramid, a beam of light was reflected from this golden blue eye that could be seen for miles around. As the age of Egypt came to a close, the priesthood removed the capstone and buried it secretly. No one knows where. But, according to the story, it will one day be rediscovered, and will be replaced on top of the pyramid. When that day comes, a "new order of the ages" will be established, which will correspond to a general spiritual awakening.

The explicitly Masonic theme of the Egyptian millennium event was astounding, considering that Freemasonry is outlawed in that country (not to mention that, having a predominantly Muslim population, the Christian dating of the year 2000 A.D. was far less meaningful than it was to Western countries). Sure enough, rumors began that this was a staged event by Masons to announce the beginning of a New World Order, which former President George H. W. Bush had alluded to during his term in office.

The head of the Giza pyramid complex, Dr. Zahi Hawass, played down suggestions that the event was linked to his own personal connections with the American New Age group, the Association for Research and Enlightenment (ARE). Instead, Hawass said, the event was based on evidence that the ancient Egyptians had a great celebration when they finished the construction of a pyramid by putting a capstone in place. He received little support from fellow Egyptian archaeologists though, who stated there was no evidence to support his claims. Ali Radwan, former head of the Egyptian Antiquities Organization, released a statement on behalf of Cairo University's Department of Egyptian Monuments, which warned about "strange religious or Masonic rituals that might be practiced on the occasion of the millennium." Once the Egyptian press got hold of the story, and public opinion in Egypt was swayed, the event was promptly cancelled.

Skull and Bones

One of the rumors which coincided with the capstone controversy was that former President George H. W. Bush had planned to be at the Giza complex for the millennium celebrations. Bush had already been singled out by conspiracy theorists for his own 'New World Order' speech, but another piece of information was equally tantalizing to them: the former President is also a member of the Yale University society 'Skull and Bones', a secret organization with distinctly Masonic overtones.

Skull and Bones was founded in 1832, notable as a time when the Craft was in decline due to the anti-Masonry surrounding the disappearance of William Morgan in 1826. Senior members choose only 15 students each year to become members. Once you are 'tapped', you become a member for life.

The skull and bones imagery appears to have originally come from the Templars. A folk tale dated to the 12th century outlines the mythical origins of the motif:

> *A great lady of Maraclea was loved by a Templar, a Lord of Sidon; but she died in her youth, and on the night of her burial, this wicked lover crept to the grave, dug up her body and violated it. Then a voice from the void bade him return in nine months time for he would find a son. He obeyed the injunction and at the appointed time he opened the grave again and found a head on the leg bones of the skeleton [the skull and crossbones]. The same voice bade him 'guard it well, for it would be the giver of all good things'...in due course, it passed into the possession of the Order.*[95]

This imagery has since become closely related to Freemasonry. Additionally, the 'Skull and Bones' fraternity at Yale shares a common motto with the Craft: *Memento Mori* (a Latin phrase meaning "remember you must die"). The amazing thing about the 'Skull and Bones' society though, is the immense power held by members, despite the size of the fraternity. If you like to play the numbers game, try this one: there are almost 300 million people living in the United States. And yet the two mainstream Presidential candidates who contested the 2004 election, John Kerry and George W. Bush, were both members of the same secret society which has only 800 or so living members: Skull and Bones.

The late Tim Russert asked each candidate about their Skull and Bones affiliation on his show 'Meet the Press', prior to the election. George W. Bush answered:

It's so secret, we can't talk about it.[96]

When Russert asked John Kerry what the significance was of both he and Bush being members of the same secret society, Kerry replied:

Not much, because it's a secret.[97]

In light of this 'dual candidacy', it is interesting to note that Antony C. Sutton introduced his seminal book *America's Secret Establishment: An Introduction to the Order of the Skull and Bones* by outlining the organization's basic philosophy for achieving absolute power:

If you can control the opposites, you dominate the nature of the outcome.

Beyond Bush and Kerry though (and not to mention former President George H. W. Bush), there are just as many 'Bonesmen' with powerful connections in the finance sector, intelligence agencies, and the halls of justice. Alexandra Robbins, author of *Secrets of the Tomb*, says that this is the primary goal of the organization: to get as many members as possible into positions of power.

For example, President George W. Bush employed five fellow Bonesmen in his first administration. One of those was William Donaldson, the head of the Securities and Exchange Commission. Society members at one time provided more than a third of the partners in financial heavyweights Morgan Stanley and Brown Brothers Harriman. At least one dozen Bonesmen can be linked to the Federal Reserve, and members also control the wealth of the Rockefeller, Carnegie, and Ford families. Other Bonesmen of note have been the 27th President of the United States, William Howard Taft, and Henry Luce, the founder of *Time Magazine*.[98]

The influence of Skull and Bones in the intelligence community and foreign affairs is especially impressive – some even claim that Bonesmen were responsible for creating the intelligence 'business' in the United States. The list of Bonesmen who have ties with the Central Intelligence Agency (C.I.A.) is formidable, and includes former President George H. W. Bush, who served as Director of the agency for a period. Considering the inclusion of Kryptos and a number of characters from the C.I.A. in *The Lost Symbol*, it's a fun fact worth keeping in mind!

In a phone call which sounds like it came straight from the pages of a Dan Brown novel, investigative journalist Ron Rosenbaum was warned against prying into the secrets of the Skull and Bones:

> *They don't like people tampering and prying. The power of Bones is incredible. They've got their hands on every lever of power in the country...it's like trying to look into the Mafia.*[99]

Additionally, Skull and Bones members have been at the center of accusations regarding the theft of the skulls of famous individuals, such as that of the well-known Native American medicine man, Geronimo. Lastly, one more interesting sidenote worth bringing up: there is somewhat of a correspondence with Dan Brown's *Angels and Demons*, as rumors abound that Bonesmen are branded with a skull and bones motif as part of their initiation. Readers will remember that in *Angels and Demons*, the killer brands Leonardo Vettra with an Illuminati ambigram.

The Dead Presidents

As we have seen, the relatively small society of Skull and Bones has amassed a large degree of power, and has 'contributed' three

Presidents of the United States. Freemasonry, which has a much larger membership, has provided even more influence in the White House. In fact, at least sixteen presidents have been confirmed as Freemasons (excluding the three Skull and Bones members):[100]

- George Washington, 1st President of the United States
- James Monroe, 5th President of the United States
- Andrew Jackson, 7th President of the United States
- James Knox Polk, 11th President of the United States
- David Rice Atchison, (ex-officio President for one day)
- James Buchanan, 15th President of the United States
- Andrew Johnson, 17th President of the United States
- James Garfield, 20th President of the United States
- William McKinley, 25th President of the United States
- Theodore Roosevelt, 26th President of the United States
- William Howard Taft, 27th President of the United States
- Warren Harding, 29th President of the United States
- Franklin D Roosevelt, 32nd President of the United States
- Harry S Truman, 33rd President of the United States
- Lyndon B Johnson, 36th President of the United States
- Gerald Ford, 40th President of the United States.

This number does not include less official relationships, such as former President Bill Clinton's involvement in the Masonic youth organization, the Order of DeMolay, or the honorary Scottish Rite membership conferred upon former President Ronald Reagan.

CHAPTER 6

THE LOST CODES

A large part of the success of Dan Brown's novels is likely due to the inclusion of puzzles, cryptograms and codes within his novels. Doing so involves the reader, as they engage their own mind trying to figure out the next clue which will drive the plot forward before the answer is revealed. As a fan of cryptography, Brown has a solid grounding in the history of this secret craft, which no doubt comes in handy during the writing of his thrillers. For instance, when writing about Leonardo Da Vinci in his previous bestseller, he employed a puzzle based on the famous painter's penchant for mirror writing.

While Kryptos sculptor James Sanborn has created ciphers that have remained uncracked for over a decade, the codes in *The Lost Symbol* are generally a lot simpler. Dan Brown certainly has some favourite ciphers, at least for presenting puzzles to the public, which he has used as devices in his previous novels and website challenges. For example, he has used the 'Caesar Box' technique on a number of occasions – a system where the message is written in a square grid vertically, and then the ciphered message read horizontally. He also employs anagrams quite a bit – not just as overt code devices as part of the plot of a novel, but also sometimes as a 'tip of the hat' to a source. For example, 'Leigh Teabing' from *The Da Vinci Code* is an anagram of the surnames of two of the authors of *Holy Blood, Holy Grail*, Michael Baigent and Richard Leigh. In *The Lost Symbol*, it seems likely that 'Nola Kaye' is a partial anagram of the first name of Elonka Dunin, a talented cryptographer and computer game developer who is recognized as an expert on Kryptos.

A quick tour of Dan Brown's favourite codes and cipher schemes offers a fun exercise in understanding the basics of cryptography, and sometimes the history behind these ciphers is as fascinating as the puzzles they conceal. So let's survey the last two thousand years of cryptography and take a look at some of Dan Brown's most often used tricks of the trade, as well as other related cipher techniques which would be worthy of inclusion in any Dan Brown novel.

Magic Squares and Sigils

Perhaps the most prominent cipher in *The Lost Symbol* is the encoding of the message 'Jeova Sanctus Unus' on the pyramid, using the magic square created by the German Renaissance master Albrecht Dürer. Leaving aside the C.I.A.'s apparent inability to crack what is basically just a bunch of scrambled letters – hardly requiring a battery of deciphering techniques as Nola Kaye suggests – Brown's decision to use a 'kamea' as part of the plot has to be praised. Not only does it offer a fun and fascinating decoding technique to the reader, but it also allows the author to explore some hidden art history which touches on Rosicrucianism and Freemasonry, and even extends to that great American Mason

Magic square (top right) in Dürer's Melencolia I

Benjamin Franklin. And, as I'll explain below, there are further curious links to American history as well.

Though Albrecht Dürer's magic square is probably the best known example, these mathematical curiosities have been with us since almost the birth of human civilization. For example, one ancient Chinese legend tells of a huge flood, during which the people were offering sacrifices to try and appease the river god. All of a sudden, "a turtle emerged from the water with a curious pattern on its shell, with patterns of circular dots arranged in a three-by-three grid on the shell, such that the sum of the numbers in each row, column and diagonal was the same: 15." The magical properties of this pattern – known as the 'Lo Shu Square' – were then used to control the river and reduce the flood.

Magic squares again came to prominence with the rise of Islamic civilization. As Europe languished in the 'Dark Ages', Islamic scientists and mathematicians preserved and enhanced the intellectual legacy of ancient China, India and Greece. They were the first to create 'recipes' for the construction of magic squares, allowing for a variety of new kameas. Like previous civilizations, they also believed that the Squares had intrinsic magical properties, and were often worn as protective amulets.

In Europe, there are only sporadic references to magic squares until the publication of Cornelius Agrippa's *De Occulta Philosophia* at the beginning of the 16th century. Agrippa's book drew on earlier magical and intellectual traditions which were coming to prominence at the birth of the Renaissance, and would become a foundational work itself for the Western magical tradition. In *De Occulta Philosophia,* Agrippa described the magical properties of seven magical squares of orders 3 to 9, associating each with one of the astrological planets. In the Western magical tradition, Dürer's 4 x 4 square is a modified version of the Square of Jupiter, while the 3 x 3 Lo Shu square, adding to 15 in each direction, is the Square of Saturn. In her book *The Occult Philosophy in the Elizabethan Age*, Renaissance scholar Dame Frances Yates puts forward sound arguments that suggest the composition of Albrecht Dürer's *Melencolia I* was directly influenced by Agrippa's book, which was circulated in manuscript form just four years before Dürer created his masterpiece.

In the Western magickal tradition, the magic squares mentioned by Agrippa are used in making 'sigils' – geometric symbols which are often inscribed on amulets and tools to instill magical properties within them (in *The Lost Symbol*, Mal'akh's body itself is covered with tattooed sigils). In *The Key of Solomon* – a magic instruction book reconstructed by occult writer S. Liddell Macgregor Mathers in 1888, from manuscripts in the British Museum – we find a section on the construction of sigils. Their creation is relatively simple: a word or name (usually of an angel or demon) is written in Hebrew, and then each letter is substituted with its numerical equivalent (see section below on Gematria). Lines are then traced through each successive number/letter of the word, as they are found on the magic square. This creates a unique symbol directly related to the magical properties associated with the magic square (as outlined by Agrippa) and also the angel, demon or spirit whose name was traced on the kamea.

Mormon Square?

Dan Brown may have stumbled onto the idea of using magic squares via Mathers' magical manual – after all, the original title for *The Lost Symbol* was *The Solomon Key*, which certainly suggests a link with Mathers' book. But there is another fascinating possibility worth discussing quickly. It is known that Dan Brown did some research into Mormonism for *The Lost Symbol* – he actually toured the Salt Lake Temple and was given access to the historic archives by church leaders. Perhaps he was interested by the fact that one of the wives of Mormon founder Joseph Smith (the early Mormon church allowed plural marriage) was Lucinda Harris – who was formerly married to William Morgan, the man whose disappearance in New York in 1826 inspired the anti-Masonic movement. But the more likely reason for Dan Brown's research into Mormonism is the strange circumstance of Joseph Smith's death.

In 1844 Smith was being held for his own protection in Carthage Jail, Illinois. Despite this measure, a mob of around 200 armed men stormed the prison, and rushed to Smith's cell, firing bullets into the door. Smith was shot several times as he attempted to escape from the mob by jumping from the second story window of his cell. It was reported that as he fell from the window, he was heard to cry the Masonic distress call "is there no help for the widow's son?"[101]

The fact that Joseph Smith used this Masonic distress call is actually no surprise – the Mormon prophet was a Freemason at the time, and numerous elements of Mormonism seem to have been influenced by Freemasonry, from its rituals to its symbols (including the all-seeing eye, the beehive, and the Sun and Moon). Poor Lucinda Harris appears to have lost two husbands to murder, with both deaths involving Freemasonry in one way or another!

One of the original sources for the Mormon-Mason link is a controversial lecture given by historian Reed Durham in 1974, with the telling title "Is There No Help For The Widow's Son?". In this lecture – which Dan Brown would no doubt have come across during his research – Durham not only explored the influence of Freemasonry on early Mormonism, but also suggested that Joseph Smith dabbled in magic, and carried on his person an amulet with a sigil based on the magic square of Jupiter:

When properly invoked, with Jupiter being very powerful and ruling in the heavens, these intelligences - by the power of ancient magic - guaranteed to the possessor of this talisman the gain of riches, and favors, and power, and love, and peace; and to confirm honors, and dignities, and councils. Talismatic magic further declared that any one who worked skillfully with this Jupiter Table would obtain the power of stimulating anyone to offer his love to the possessor of the talisman, whether from a friend, brother, relative, or even any female. Whether or not Joseph Smith was first introduced to this kind of magic through Masonry is not known at present.

Regardless of whether this was how Dan Brown came to include magic squares in *The Lost Symbol*, the further link he made with other aspects of his research – via the wordplay of the coded message "Order 8 Franklin Square" – was one of the highpoints of the novel.

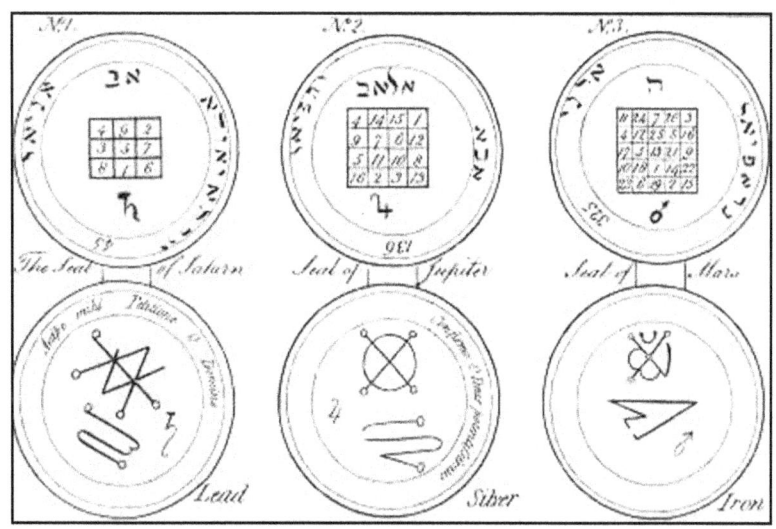

Talismans and sigils of Saturn, Jupiter and Mars respectively

Franklin Squares (and Circles)

Including Dürer's magic square in *The Lost Symbol* was a brilliant move, but to then use that as the basis for jumping to the magic square of Benjamin Franklin – already related to the story through his influence in both Freemasonry and the founding of the United States – was, quite simply, a masterstroke.

Benjamin Franklin discussed his hobby of constructing magic squares in a letter written in 1752, which can be found in Volume 2 of *The Writings of Benjamin Franklin* (under the title "The Arithmetical Curiosity") :

> *Being one day in the country, at the house of our common friend, the late learned Mr. Logan, he shewed me a folio French book, filled with magic squares…in which he said the author had discovered great ingenuity and dexterity in the management of numbers; and, though several other foreigners had distinguished themselves in the same way, he did not recollect that any one Englishman had done any thing of the kind remarkable.*

> *…I then confessed to him, that in my younger days, having once some leisure, (which I still think I might have employed more usefully) I had amused myself in making these kind of magic squares, and, at length, had acquired such a knack at it, that I could fill the cells of any magic square, of reasonable size, with a series of numbers as fast as I could write them, disposed in such a manner, as that the sums of every row, horizontal, perpendicular, or diagonal, should be equal; but not being satisfied with these, which I looked on as common and easy things, I had imposed on myself more difficult tasks, and succeeded in making other magic squares, with a variety of properties, and much more curious.*

Upon Logan's request, Franklin brought with him on his next visit the kamea he had created. Though not properly 'Magic' – the diagonals did not add to the same amount as the columns and rows – it did have other even more impressive aspects. While each row and column of the 8 x 8 square added to 260, any half column or row added to exactly 130. And though the diagonals didn't sum to 260, the 'bent diagonals' did (half a diagonal which is then mirrored on the other half of the square, rather than continuing straight).

Logan then showed Franklin an old book written by Michel Stifelius, which contained a 16 x 16 square, commenting that creating such a huge square must have been "a work of great labour." Not wanting to be intellectually outdone, Franklin went home and made that night a magic square of 16. This new square had all the properties of his 8 x 8 square, plus the additional feature of every 4 x 4 square grid within it summing to 2056, just as the 16 squares of each row and column did. No doubt pleased with his work, Franklin sent the newly constructed square to Logan the next morning, and in his recounting of Logan's reaction we get a real glimpse of this great American's impish sense of humor:

> *This I sent to our friend the next morning, who, after some days, sent it back in a letter, with these words: "I return to thee thy astonishing or most stupendous piece of the magical square, in which"...but the compliment is too extravagant, and therefore, for his sake, as well as my own, I ought not to repeat it. Nor is it necessary; for I make no question but you will readily allow this square of 16 to be the most magically magical of any magic square ever made by any magician.*

Not content with large magic squares, Benjamin Franklin also created a Magic Circle, "consisting of 8 concentric circles, and 8 radial rows, filled with a series of numbers, from 12 to

75, inclusive, so disposed as that the numbers of each circle, or each radial row, being added to the central number 12, they made exactly 360, the number of degrees in a circle."

Lastly, one last piece of magic square trivia. Given the recurrence of the number 33 in *The Lost Symbol*, it's a shame that Dan Brown didn't make a quick reference to the well-known magic square found on the façade of the Sagrada Família church in Barcelona. Designed by sculptor Josep Subirachs, the rows and columns of this 4 × 4 kamea total not to 34, as is usual for the Square of Jupiter, but to 33! It must be admitted that to do so, some numbers in the square are repeated – so strictly speaking it is not a normal magic square – but it still would have made a fun reference.

The Masonic Cipher

Manly Hall mentions in *The Secret Teachings of All Ages* that Freemasons were known to have used a number of secret alphabets, including 'Angelic' and 'Celestial' writing. However, one secret alphabet in particular was used so much by the Craft that it came to be known as the Masonic Cipher. Also called the Pigpen Cipher, this technique was used widely by 18th century Masons for keeping private correspondence secret, though its simplicity means it is virtually obsolete in the modern age. Except, of course, for Dan Brown, who has used it on multiple occasions now – most recently, as the method of enciphering the text of the magic square on the pyramid in *The Lost Symbol*. At least Brown recognizes the simplicity of this cipher, as he has Robert Langdon say that "Anyone could decipher this engraving…It's not very sophisticated."

The Masonic Cipher substitutes a symbol for each letter of the alphabet, with the symbol being a description of where the letter is placed on the 'pigpen grids' (a noughts and crosses grid of 9

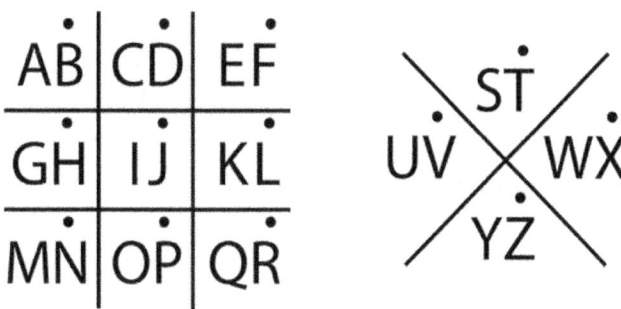

'English' Masonic Cipher example

squares, and also two diagonal lines forming a grid of 4 triangles. Two letters are placed in each grid space (13 grid spaces x 2 = 26 letters of the alphabet), with the second letter being designated by both the shape of the grid space as well as a dot.

Note that there are many different ways of laying out the letters on the pigpen grid, so each will encode differently. The two most common are the 'English method', whereby the letters are placed in the square and diagonal grids two at a time ('ab', 'cd' etc.), and the 'American method', which runs through the alphabet one grid space at a time (thus typical grid squares are 'an', 'bo' etc). Dan Brown uses a third method in *The Lost Symbol*: the grid of 9 squares is filled twice over ('a' to 'i', then 'j' to 'r'), followed by the diagonal grid of 4 triangles twice over ('s' to 'v', then 'w' to 'z').

BACONIAN CIPHERS

Sir Francis Bacon is mentioned numerous times in *The Lost Symbol* – the British politician, scientist, and philosopher who, as we have seen, was rumoured to be involved with Rosicrucianism and the Invisible College, and who also authored *The New Atlantis*, a Utopian tract which many think served as the blueprint for the American 'experiment'. But Bacon was also deeply interested in cryptography, and used a number of cipher methods and personal codes in his writings. Perhaps not just 'his' writings either – some alternative history researchers attribute the works of Shakespeare to him, on the basis of numerous similarities.

The esoteric expert Manly P. Hall devotes a number of chapters to Bacon in his masterwork (and Dan Brown favourite), *The Secret Teachings of All Ages*. One chapter deals with the Bacon-Shakespeare theory, while another delves into his cryptographic methods, relating it to Bacon's Rosicrucian leanings. Dan Brown is definitely familiar with Baconian ciphers, as in *The Da Vinci Code* he writes that:

> Langdon had once worked on a series of Baconian manuscripts that contained epigraphical ciphers in which certain lines of code were clues as to how to decipher the other lines.[102]

In *The Secret Teachings of All Ages,* Manly Hall outlines a number of different cipher systems employed by Francis Bacon:

Biliteral Ciphers:

Bacon's most famous contribution to cryptography is his 'biliteral cipher', first described in *De Augmentis Scientiarum* in 1605. Bacon thought that obvious ciphers, where the passage was an unreadable jumble of letters, only encouraged people to investigate further. Instead he thought that ciphers should "be without suspicion" – that is, the person reading the encoded message should not be aware a cipher is present, unless properly trained to do so. This technique is often referred to as steganography.

Bacon's biliteral cipher is based around the use of just two letters, 'a' and 'b', which are used in five-character combinations to designate each letter of the alphabet. For example, the letter 'f' might be ciphered as 'aabba' in the biliteral system. Bacon's cipher is an early example of the binary code which now rules our world, via computers, and is also a precursor to the dots and dashes of Morse code.

Bacon's biliteral cipher combined this idea of binary coding with a process of font encoding, whereby two different font types would be used when publishing a manuscript. One font was the 'a' font, the other the 'b', and as such the five-letter biliteral 'words' could be encoded into any text to be printed – no matter what its literary content – by simply manipulating the fonts. To explain it simplistically, let's use a lower case font as our 'a', and upper case as the 'b' font. This will of course make the cipher blatantly obvious – proper use entails keeping upper and lower case as normal and employing only subtle differences between the fonts.

In our example, we will use five arbitrary letter combinations to designate the letters C,D,E,O and S:

C = aaaba
D = aaabb
E = aabaa
O = abbab
S = baaab

Using the passage 'Francis Bacon was Shakespeare', our encoded message would be published like this:

FRAnCIs bAcON Was SHaKEsPEAre

Here's the explanation of how the cipher works: separating the sentence into five letter groups (with one left over which we will ignore), we can see the parallel between the font encoding and the biliteral cipher words:

FRAnC IsbAc ONWas SHaKE sPEAre
aaaba   abbab   aaabb   aabaa   baaab
  C   O   D   E   S

Our encoded word is therefore – CODES. As mentioned above, our example is intentionally obvious. If you would like to test your powers of observation, a more realistic example of using two different fonts might look like this:

Francis Bacon was Shakespeare

In *De Augmentis Scientiarum*, Bacon actually used an example where even the encoded word was replaced by a simple substitution cipher, just to further complicate the decoding sequence and thereby discourage crackers.[103] Have you spotted any odd typography in *The Lost Symbol*?

The Alchemical Cipher:

The alchemical cipher is a literal cipher – that is, one to do with the arrangement or combination of letters of the alphabet.[104] Manly Hall gives a couple of examples of this sort of cryptogram, both of which are composed of circular diagrams combined with words. By reading the first letter of each word, a hidden code is revealed.

For example, an alchemical cryptogram composed by the Jesuit scholar Athanasius Kircher shows a number of Latin words running around its circular perimeter: *Sola, Vera, Laudat, Philosophia, Homines, Veritatis, Rectae*. If the reader picks out the first letter of each word they will find the word SVLPHVR – 'sulphur', once the 'V' is transposed to a 'u'. Continuing with the rest of the words on the diagram, the final decoded combination of words is *Sulphur Fixum Est Sol*, or 'Fixed Sulphur is Gold' – a definite alchemical phrase, and as such worthy of hiding from

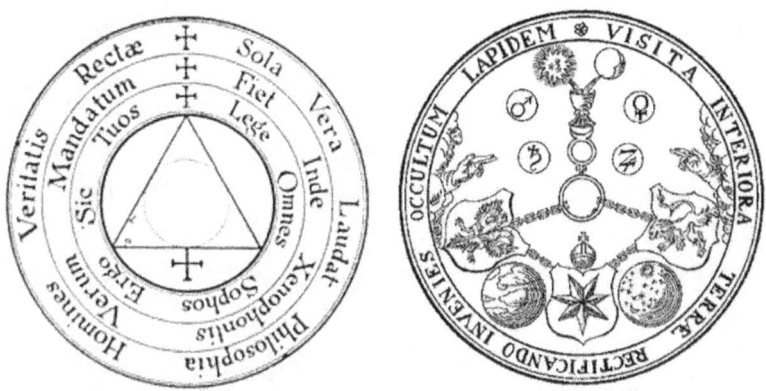

Kircher's SVLPHVR Cipher (left) and Masonic VITRIOL Cipher (right)

'profane eyes'. This technique is similar to the 'acrostic', whereby the first letter of each line in a manuscript is read to reveal the hidden message. Another alchemical cipher is mentioned briefly in *The Lost Symbol* – the word VITRIOL, found in the Chamber of Reflection, which stands for "Visita Interiora Terrae, Rectificando Invenies Occultum Lapidem" (Visit the interior of the earth, and by rectifying, you will find the hidden stone). Like the above cipher, it is sometimes written around a circular talisman.

We can see in the above two ciphers a possible relationship with the anagram of MASON found on the Great Seal. Though most rule this out as a simple coincidence, the geometric overlay of the Seal of Solomon on the Great Seal reveals the anagram from the curved text, 'for those with eyes to see', in a very similar manner to the above two examples. We might just have to be careful though, or Robert Langdon might consider us one of those "crazy conspiracy theorists"…

Pictorial Ciphers:

Manly Hall describes pictorial ciphers as "any picture or drawing with other than its obvious meaning", and categorizes the diagrams of alchemists as such.[105] They can take many forms – the number of bricks in a wall, the fold of a person's clothes, the position of the subject's fingers, and structures in the form of letters (such as the alleged "M" found within *The Last Supper*).

One such enciphered code was the initials 'AA', which can be seen in a number of Rosicrucian diagrams and headpieces, including some works of Shakespeare, and which has particular meaning for those in the Rosicrucian tradition. It can also be found in some of Bacon's philosophical works. Another favourite of Bacon's was, fittingly enough, the image of a hog. We could probably include the 'symbature' of Albrecht Dürer, mentioned in *The Lost Symbol*, within this category.

Numerical Ciphers:

The simplest numerical cipher is one in which the letters of the alphabet are substituted with their corresponding numbers: A=1, B=2, C=3 etc. In the Baconian system, both 'I' and 'J' are equivalent to 9, and 'U' and 'V' are both 20. In our case, the keyword CODES would thus become 3-14-4-5-18. The keyword could be further obscured by inserting a pre-arranged number of non-significant characters – for example, inserting one 'fake' number between each real one: 3-2-14-20-4-8-5-10-18.

Important words in this system would then also become recognizable by a single number: the sum of their components. For example, using our keyword CODES, we have 3+14+4+5+18 = 44. This is of course using the simplest version of the numerical cipher – tables of correspondence between letters and arbitrary number values can be developed for a more complex cipher.

Manly Hall points out that authors of numerical cryptograms can also create a 'signature number' from the numerical value of their own names.[106] For example, Francis Bacon is said to have regularly used the number 33 – the numerical equivalent of

'Bacon'. The author of a coded message can therefore 'sign' his work by an in-joke, such as some glaring error on that particular page number, word number or combination of both.

Dan Brown appears to have enjoyed using the number 33 as well in *The Lost Symbol*. Apart from the obvious link to Scottish Rite Freemasonry, Brown seems to have had a little Baconian-style fun with the number himself – the opening of *The Lost Symbol* is at 8.33 pm, there are 133 chapters in the book, and on page 333 the number 33 is repeated numerous times. If that's not enough to convince you, then perhaps add up the three individual numbers in the release date of *The Lost Symbol*: 09-15-09. What do you think – coincidence?

To compare: Bacon also employed the number 287 as a personal motif. In his *Advancement of Learning*, there are 287 letters on the frontispiece, 287 letters on the Dedication page, and 287 letters on the page numbered 215 – which is actually falsely numbered and is really page 287.[107]

Kabbalah and Magick

Both Rosicrucians and Freemasons are known to have been influenced by the system of Jewish mysticism called the Kabbalah. The numerical cipher mentioned above has its roots in the Kabbalistic technique of Gematria. Hebrew mystics saw great truths in the numerical equivalent of words, even to the point where the sum of two words which equaled another would constitute a definite relationship. For example, the Hebrew words *aheva* ('love') and *echod* ('one') are both numerically equivalent in Gematria to the number 13. The name of God, *YHVH* or

Jehovah, is equal to 26. Thus, God = one love.[108] A number of ancient religious traditions have similar systems – one magic square devised by Islamic mathematicians added to 66 in each direction, which was the numerical equivalent of 'Allah'.

A second technique, the Notarikon, is a system of creating a new word from the components of a group of other words. Many of our modern-day acronyms basically fit into this system (minus the Hebrew language aspect of course). A good example of the Notarikon is a biblical word known to most of us, 'Amen'. Amen is a composite of three words: *Al*, *Melech* and *Neh-eh-mahn* (A.M.N.) meaning 'God is our faithful king'.[109]

The third Kabbalistic method we should mention is called Temurah. This is basically a straight substitution cipher, with letters transposed into corresponding characters according to a set system.[110] The Atbash cipher, used by the Jewish sect known as the Essenes, is one of a number of methods described by Temurah. It is mentioned in *The Da Vinci Code*, where Dan Brown describes it as "one of the oldest codes known to man." Dr Hugh Schonfield first proposed the decryption of the mysterious Templar word 'Baphomet' using the Atbash Cipher. This cipher is a straight substitution between two Hebrew alphabets, one written forward and the other in reverse (so in modern English, A and Z are interchangeable, B and Y, C and X, and so on). For example, Bible scholars found that applying the Atbash to the mysterious location of 'Scheschach' resulted in the more recognizable 'Babel'. This technique is referred to as a 'mono-alphabetic substitution cipher', and similar ciphers were successfully used right up until the Renaissance. If you ever want to encipher (or decipher) a message in an Atbash-like cipher, a simple method is to write the first 13 letters of the alphabet (A to M) from left to right, and then the second 13 immediately below the first line from right to left. This will give you a simple chart to find the corresponding coded letter for enciphering and deciphering.

Revolutionary Codes

At times of war, there is a desperate need to keep many things secret from the enemy. It is no surprise, therefore, that many of America's Founding Fathers are known to have used various codes and techniques during the American Revolution. Seeing as *The Lost Symbol* referenced much of the secret history of this formative part of American history, it's worth taking a look at the cipher systems of the Revolutionaries.

The Culper Ring was a spy ring organized under the orders of George Washington in 1778, tasked with infiltrating British-controlled New York City. Washington himself supplied the Culpers with a special substance with which they could report back to him secretly: invisible ink. Supplied to him by Sir James Jay in London, Washington was said to have reported back to Jay "acknowledging their great utility, and requesting further supplies." The "stain", as Washington called it, was also used by Jay himself to transmit "to America the first authentic account which Congress received, of the determination of the British Ministry to reduce the colonies to unconditional submission":

> *My method of communication was this: to prevent the suspicion which might arise were I to write to my brother John only, who was a member of Congress, I write with black ink a short letter to him, and likewise to 1 or 2 other persons of the family, none exceeding 3 or 4 lines in black ink. The residue of the blank paper I filled up, invisibly, with such intelligence and matters as I thought would be useful to the American cause...In this invisible writing I sent to [Benjamin] Franklin and [Silas] Deane, by the mail from London to Paris, a plan of the intended Expedition under Burgoyne from Canada.*

James Lovell – who as we have seen was the chair of the second panel put in charge of designing the Great Seal – is mentioned by American military historian David Kahn as the "Father of American Cryptanalysis". Lovell's expertise in deciphering coded messages may have been crucial in the outcome of the war – in 1781 he broke some intercepted cipher-texts, which allowed the Revolutionaries to read numerous other messages and helped to win some decisive battles. Lovell himself favoured a numerical version of the well known Vigenère cipher (a polyalphabetic system, where the individual letters of a repeating key word are used to do a Caesar shift on each letter of the message to be encoded), and also 'book codes'. Book codes were a common cipher method of the time, also being used by other prominent individuals such as Benedict Arnold.

Arnold's first book code was based on Volume 1 of Blackstone's *Commentaries*, a classic legal tome. Each word of the message to be deciphered would be represented by three numbers: the first would point the decipherer to a page in the book, the second the line on that page, and the third the number of words to count along that line. However, Arnold and his co-conspirators ran into problems with the amount of time it took to find each word, so they modified their choice of book: they instead decided on a dictionary.

While in France, Benjamin Franklin used a special numerical substitution cipher that he devised to send confidential messages. He wrote out a long passage in French, and then assigned each letter in the passage to its numerical place. To illustrate: using "la maison", the letter 'l' would become '1', 'a' becomes '2', 'm' becomes '3', and so on. If we wanted to send the word "snail", it would therefore become 6,8,2,5,1 – or, as there are two instances of the letter 'a' in "la maison", also 6,8,4,5,1. In Franklin's case, there were more than 100 different numbers just for the letter 'e'!

The Jefferson Wheel Cipher

Jefferson, like Benjamin Franklin, was a keen inventor. While serving as the United States Secretary of State under the Presidency of George Washington, Jefferson created his own cipher method. As mail at the time was very insecure, secrecy was paramount when communicating affairs of the nation. Jefferson's idea was the encryption of a message using a 'wheel cipher'.

Jefferson's invention consisted of a number of flat wooden disks, each around ½ inch in thickness, layered together using an iron spindle through their center (to visualize this, imagine a spindle of blank CDs on its side...only the CDs are much thicker than normal). The complete alphabet was inscribed on the edge of each disk in random order. By spelling out the cipher message across one row by turning each disk into place, twenty-five separate encoded phrases were therefore available to be chosen from the other rows on the disk.[111]

Someone with the same arrangement of disks and letters would then be able to spell out the encoded phrase on their cipher wheel, and then scan the other rows for one that made sense. Jefferson's invention was well ahead of its time: David Kahn describes it as "far and away the most advanced devised in its day...so well conceived was it that today, more than a century and a half of rapid technological progress after its invention, it remains in use."

Beyond the 'Jefferson Wheel Cipher', the third President of the United States also used the well-known Vigenère method of encoding messages. Indeed, with the penchant that the Founding Fathers of the United States had for cryptography, it's almost a shame that he didn't include more references to these historical cipher techniques in *The Lost Symbol*.

Right Before Your Eyes

Now that you've finished this primer on some of the cipher systems which relate to *The Lost Symbol*, you might like to put some of your new-found knowledge to the test. Just as he did with *The Da Vinci Code*, Dan Brown has hidden some coded messages on the cover of *The Lost Symbol* (hardcover US edition only). One decodes to a phone number which readers could ring to try and win a signed copy of the book (unfortunately for latecomers, all have been won at this late stage). Others give short messages relevant to the topics in *The Lost Symbol* – and there may still be a hidden message to be found. Nothing too groundbreaking, but it's certainly a fun exercise. If you're stuck, or don't have the time, see Appendix 1 at the back of this book for a full run-down on these hidden cover codes.

CHAPTER 7

MYSTERIES OF THE MIND

In *The Lost Symbol*, Dan Brown introduces the unexpected subject of 'Noetic Sciences', which he says has recently been "opening new doors of understanding into the power of the human mind." As mentioned on the opening page of the novel, the Institute of Noetic Sciences (IONS) is indeed a real organization, and Dan Brown's summation of their research is, quite bizarrely, spot on. However, perhaps one of the more interesting facts about IONS was not mentioned in *The Lost Symbol*. The Institute was founded by Apollo 14 astronaut Edgar Mitchell in 1973, after he had a mystical experience while returning from the Moon in 1971:

> *Suddenly from behind the rim of the moon, in long, slow-motion moments of immense majesty, there emerges a sparkling blue and white jewel, a light, delicate sky-blue sphere laced with slow swirling veils of white, rising gradually like a small pearl in a thick sea of black mystery. It takes more than a moment to fully realize this is Earth – home.*

> *On the return trip home, gazing through 240,000 miles of space toward the stars and the planet from which I had come, I suddenly experienced the universe as intelligent, loving, harmonious.*

> *...When I went to the moon, I was as pragmatic a test pilot, engineer, and scientist as any of my colleagues. But when I saw the planet Earth floating in the vastness of space...the presence of divinity became almost palpable, and I knew that life in the universe was not just an accident based on random processes.*

Mitchell's heavenly epiphany instilled in him a determination to "broaden the knowledge of the nature and potentials of mind and consciousness, and to apply that knowledge to the enhancement of human well-being and the quality of life on the planet," leading him to found IONS two years later. The name of the organization is based on the Greek word *noetikos*, meaning "inner/intuitive knowing."

Over the ensuing three decades, the Institute of Noetic Science – which is situated on a 200-acre property north of San Francisco – has worked with highly-qualified researchers throughout the world, investigating the nature of consciousness from a number of cutting-edge perspectives. The organization was involved in some of the first research into 'Remote Viewing', conducted by Harold Puthoff and Russell Targ at Stanford Research Institute, and which subsequently morphed into the U.S. Army's "Stargate" program (mentioned by Dan Brown in *The Lost Symbol*). IONS has also collaborated with researchers at Princeton University on anomalous interactions between consciousness and matter; on a program investigating the efficacy of visualization therapy for terminally ill cancer patients; and offered grants to researchers testing the power of prayer and intention on healing. IONS President James O'Dea set out the current mission of the organization recently, and it sounds very similar to the theme of impending transformation enunciated in *The Lost Symbol*: "There is a clear need for a bold new synthesis of the implications of what we're discovering about the nature of consciousness with equally bold application," according to O'Dea. "IONS will be a nexus which skillfully demonstrates how worldview transformation can advance greater health, creativity, and peace for all human beings."

Frontier Science

For many people, the research and aims of the Institute of Noetic Sciences may seem rather 'New Age' and speculative. Before dismissing these ideas out of hand though, one might consider the following remarks from a respected scholar:

> *Using the standards applied to any other area of science, it is concluded that psychic functioning has been well-established. The statistical results of the studies examined are far beyond what is expected by chance...there is little benefit to continuing experiments designed to offer proof, since there is little more to be offered to anyone who does not accept the current collection of data.*[112]

This is the extraordinary summation of University of California statistician Professor Jessica Utts. The remarks were made in her review of formerly classified government-sponsored research into 'psi' abilities, in particular the ability to 'see at a distance' – known in the past as 'travelling clairvoyance', and in modern times as 'remote viewing'. Utts was part of a 2-person review commissioned by the US Congress to evaluate the mass of experiments undertaken over the course of two decades. Her partner in this review was noted skeptic Professor Ray Hyman. Hyman's conclusions differed slightly from Utts, although in a telling way – he determined that the...

> ...*experiments are well-designed and the investigators have taken pains to eliminate the known weaknesses in previous parapsychological research. In addition, I cannot provide suitable candidates for what flaws, if any, might be present. Just the same, it is impossible in principle to say that any particular experiment or experimental series is completely free from flaws.*[113]

Of course, the critical thinker would notice that Hyman's sole 'criticism' is in fact a statement on scientific experiments in general, and in no way is the validity of the positive data in doubt because of his comments. Utts' specifically mentions this fact (judging by the "standards applied to any other area of science"), and as such Hyman's statement is indicative of a man who sees results that don't agree with his worldview, and therefore assumes that although he can't see the error...there simply must be one. If anything, such words coming from Hyman's mouth are the closest one would expect for a confirmation of psi effects from a heavyweight 'skeptic'.

Remote viewing is classed as a type of extrasensory perception (ESP), and describes a protocol in which a person is able to describe in detail activities and locations ('targets') blocked from ordinary perception. The effect does not appear to be influenced by distance, with similar results in experiments over a few meters to a range of thousands of kilometers. An illustrative example of a modern remote viewer is former police commissioner and ex-vice-mayor of Burbank, California, the late Pat Price. In his first informal remote-viewing experiment he was amazingly accurate, down to being able to read the labels on folders locked in filing cabinets. Price displayed an excellent ability to remote view over many experiments, to the point where experimenter Dr. Hal Puthoff remarked that Price's accuracy "began to raise a paranoid fear in me that perhaps Price and the division director were in collusion on this experiment to see if I could detect chicanery".[114]

Jessica Utts' conclusion on research into remote viewing is an important step forward in acknowledging that we still have a lot to learn about the nature of the universe and the extent of human abilities. Other recent research serves to reinforce this fact. At Princeton University, Professor of Physics Robert Jahn and psychologist Brenda Dunne have produced evidence that humans can influence the behaviour of physical devices through thought alone – 'mind over matter' as it were.[115] The work of Jahn and Dunne at the Princeton Engineering Anomalies Research (PEAR) lab was mentioned in *The Lost Symbol*, and Dunne may even have served as the model for the character of Trish Dunne in the book (if so, I wonder what she thinks about the ultimate fate of Katherine Solomon's offsider?!). Jahn and Dunne have also conducted experiments in remote viewing with positive results. After 28 years of research, the lab shut down in 2007 – because, in Robert Jahn's words...

> ...there's no reason to stay and generate more of the same data. If people don't believe us after all the results we've produced, then they never will... It's time for a new era; for someone to figure out what the implications of our results are for human culture.

During the 1990s, scientists at the PEAR lab and the Consciousness Research Laboratory at the University of Nevada worked on a phenomenon which they call 'field consciousness'.

The Global Consciousness Project (GCP) was begun in 1998, and conducted experiments which studied the effect of major world events on random-number generating machines. Maintained by an international team of around 100 researchers, the GCP's data suggests that the 'group consciousness' of large amounts of people watching live television broadcasts – such as the Academy Awards and the O.J. Simpson verdict – can have an effect on the physical world.[116]

Dean Radin, who worked at the Consciousness Research Laboratory – and is now Senior Scientist at the Institute of Noetic Sciences – has also accumulated data which suggest that humans carry the ability to feel emotion before an event occurs – a branch of precognition termed presentiment.[117] Experiments such as these have been replicated by independent laboratories, and have satisfied the requirements for validity of any 'orthodox' science hypotheses.

Returning to remote viewing, and Dan Brown's assertion that psychic skills such as this were once well-understood by ancient people, it may be worthwhile taking a closer look at this phenomenon throughout history.

Counting the Sands

The remote viewing research mentioned above has its parallels in anecdotes throughout history. Herodotus, that most celebrated of ancient historians, recorded the following account of an 'experiment' by Croesus, King of Lydia, circa 550 BC. Croesus dispatched messengers to the great oracles of the time, in order that he could assess their abilities:

> *The messengers who were despatched to make trial of the oracles were given the following instructions: they were to*

keep count of the days from the time of their leaving Sardis, and, reckoning from that date, on the hundredth day they were to consult the oracles, and to inquire of them what Croesus the son of Alyattes, king of Lydia, was doing at that moment. The answers given them were to be taken down in writing, and brought back to him. None of the replies remain on record except that of the oracle at Delphi. There, the moment that the Lydians entered the sanctuary, and before they put their questions, the Pythoness thus answered them in hexameter verse:-

"I can count the sands, and I can measure the ocean; I have ears for the silent, and know what the dumb man meaneth; Lo! on my sense there striketh the smell of a shell-covered tortoise, Boiling now on a fire, with the flesh of a lamb, in a cauldron. Brass is the vessel below, and brass the cover above it."

These words the Lydians wrote down at the mouth of the Pythoness as she prophesied, and then set off on their return to Sardis. When all the messengers had come back with the answers which they had received, Croesus undid the rolls, and read what was written in each. Only one approved itself to him, that of the Delphic oracle. This he had no sooner heard than he instantly made an act of adoration, and accepted it as true, declaring that the Delphic was the only really oracular shrine, the only one that had discovered in what way he was in fact employed. For on the departure of his messengers he had set himself to think what was most impossible for any one to conceive of his doing, and then, waiting till the day agreed on came, he acted as he had determined. He took a tortoise and a lamb, and cutting them in pieces with his own hands, boiled them both together in a brazen cauldron, covered over with a lid which was also of brass.

Herodotus' account describes the oracle of Delphi observing happenings at a remote location *sans* the usual means of perception. While it can hardly be taken as proof of remote viewing in antiquity, it does contain startling similarities to the phenomenon. And it is not a lone example.

The 18th century Christian mystic Emanuel Swedenborg first swept into the public eye after a notorious incident which occurred in 1759. Swedenborg was dining with friends in the Swedish city of Gothenburg, when he became agitated and withdrew from the table for a time, retiring to the garden. Upon his return, he announced that a great fire had broken out in his hometown of Stockholm – some 300 miles distant – and feared that his residence would be consumed by the inferno. Later that evening, he happily announced "Thank God! The fire is extinguished the third door from my house". It was not until two days later that a messenger arrived from Stockholm with details of the fire that Swedenborg had mentioned. His account was accurate.[118]

Techniques of Ecstasy

Perhaps the original and greatest exponent of 'seeing at a distance', the shaman, is an archetypal figure seen in most ancient cultures. The respected anthropologist Mircea Eliade saw shamanism as the "technique of ecstasy" (not the modern definition of ecstasy, but "a trance state in which intense absorption in divine or cosmic matters is accompanied by loss of sense perception and voluntary control"[119]). The shaman specializes in a trance during which his soul apparently leaves his body and ascends to the sky or descends to the underworld.[120] There are numerous allusions to this sort of technique in *The*

Lost Symbol, including Robert Langdon's experience in the 'Total Liquid Ventilation' tank where he seems to 'remote view' Mal'akh walking the streets of Washington, D.C. while in 'suspended animation' miles away.

While there is little surviving documentation on ancient shamanistic journeys, there are modern examples which offer a glimpse into the abilities of these ancient magicians. A report by a missionary, Father Trilles, working with the pygmies of equatorial Africa, suggests that not only were shamans able to 'see', but also communicate with others. Father Trilles had asked a native who was apparently visiting a village four days walk distant, to transmit a message to a person there named Esab' Ava requesting ammunition. He was allowed to be present during the departure preparations, and must have been astonished at what followed. He reported that the native:

> *...first smeared his body with a special mixture...then he lit a fire and walked around it, saying prayers to the spirits of the air and the guardian spirits of the magic brotherhood. He then fell into a state of ecstasy, showed the whites of his eyes, his skin became insensitive and his limbs rigid. It was ten o'clock the next day when he came out of his trance, and during that time Father Trilles had not left his side. When he awoke, the man gave some details about the reunion at which he had been present and then, without being asked, said: "Your message has been carried out. Esab' Ava has been warned. He will set out this morning and will bring you the powder and the cartridges." Three days later...Esab' Ava arrived at the village with the goods.*[121]

This 'special mixture' which the native smeared his body with was no doubt an entheogen (also known as hallucinogens).

Smearing the body with such an ointment to induce magical journeys was a tradition known across many cultures and throughout history. In 'Metamorphoses', the ancient writer Lucius Apuleius seeks from a witch a magical ointment which would transform him into a bird, in order that he could fly through the air.[122] And anthropologist Michael Harner's research into European witchcraft led to the discovery that witches rubbed their bodies with a salve containing entheogenic plants  such as henbane, mandrake and deadly nightshade to assist in 'travelling' to the Sabbat. Indeed, Harner has put forth solid evidence that the now legendary use of a broomstick by witches served a double purpose – as an applicator for the atropine-containing plants to the sensitive vaginal membranes, as well as providing the witch with the helpful imagery of a physical device which they could use as transport to the otherworldly realm (pitchforks, baskets and bowls were also used).[123]

While there is a vast amount of literature available on the use of entheogens to facilitate altered states of consciousness, it is hardly the only method used. Other techniques included sonic driving (e.g. drumming), kinetic stimulation and hyperventilation (e.g. ritual dancing), meditation, trance, sensory deprivation (such as Robert Langdon's experience in the tank), ritualization (ritual magick, as practiced by Mal'akh) and extreme temperature conditions (seen most typically in the Native American sweat lodges). Cultures throughout history have used such techniques to access the mysterious hidden abilities of the human mind. Sometimes these involved psi-like effects, as mentioned above. On other occasions though, the access given was to a far more mystical realm – that of the afterlife.

The Subtle Body

Perhaps the most fascinating branch of consciousness research is that concerned with the question of whether humans have a 'soul', and if it survives into an afterlife. While this area is far more subjective, and faces obvious difficulties in providing evidence (being closer in many respects to metaphysics than physics), there is still a great deal of material which is of interest. It's worth covering here as Dan Brown mentions a number of times that Katherine Solomon was researching the existence of the human soul.

Now before exploring the topic further, we should quickly put to bed the story about how Katherine Solomon came up with the novel idea of weighing a person during their death, to see if it would be possible to measure the departing soul. Alas, poor Katherine was beaten to the punch on this by more than a century. In 1907 a Massachusetts physician, Dr. Duncan MacDougall, weighed six patients while they were in the process of dying from tuberculosis. He found an average weight loss of 21 grams after death in humans, whilst similar experiments on dogs showed no change. Dr. MacDougall postulated therefore that humans had a soul that left the body after death, while dogs have no soul. Though his experiments could have had numerous flaws – and ethical restrictions would prohibit similar modern-day investigations (sorry Katherine!) – the '21 grams' attribution has stuck. These days, modern research into the possibility of the survival of death tends to focus on two areas: the testing of information received from 'psychic mediums', and investigation of the Near Death Experience (NDE).

Modern research into mediums has largely been done in two projects, one by Dr. Gary Schwartz at the University of Virginia, the other by Dr. Julie Beischel at the Windbridge Institute, who previously worked with Dr. Schwartz on a program known as VERITAS. Most readers would be surprised to know that when they published their results in a paper titled "Anomalous Information Reception by Research Mediums Demonstrated Using a Novel Triple-Blind Protocol," Schwartz and Beischel found that even under stringent conditions, "evidence for anomalous information reception can be obtained." Research is continuing in this area.

Scientific investigation of Near Death Experiences has been ongoing over the past thirty years, but perhaps the most exciting development is the research currently being undertaken by the Human Consciousness Project, an international consortium of multidisciplinary scientists and physicians who have joined forces to research consciousness and its relationship with the brain. Doctors at 25 hospitals in the United States and United Kingdom will study 1500 survivors of life-threatening medical situations, to see if people with no heartbeat or brain activity can have what is known as an 'Out-of-Body' experience (OBE). Hidden targets will be placed in the resuscitation room, in positions that can only be viewed from up near the ceiling. If any survivor of an NDE reports a hidden target, this will go a long way to showing that the human soul can wander away from the physical body during an OBE.

Near death experiences first came to public prominence with the publication of Dr Raymond Moody's bestseller, *Life After Life*, in which he found that many stories of NDE subjects shared common elements. From this Moody was able to construct a 'typical NDE' (although he points out that no NDE contains all the details included):

> *A man is dying and, as he reaches the point of greatest physical distress, he hears himself pronounced dead by his doctor. He begins to hear an uncomfortable noise, a loud ringing or buzzing, and at the same time feels himself moving very rapidly through a long dark tunnel. After this, he suddenly*

Detail from Hieronymus Bosch's "Ascent of the Blessed", thought to depict an NDE

finds himself outside of his own physical body, but still in the immediate physical environment, and he sees his own body from a distance, as though he is a spectator. He watches the resuscitation attempt from this unusual vantage point and is in a state of emotional upheaval.

After a while, he collects himself and becomes more accustomed to his odd condition. He notices he still has a "body", but one of a very different nature and with very different powers from the physical body he has left behind. Soon other things begin to happen. Others come to meet and to help him. He glimpses the spirits of relatives and friends who have already died, and a loving warm spirit of a kind he has never encountered before – a being of light – appears before him. This being asks him a question, nonverbally, to make him evaluate his life and helps him along by showing him a panoramic, instantaneous playback of the major events of his life. At some point he finds himself approaching some sort of barrier or border, apparently representing the limit between earthly life and the next life. Yet, he finds that he must go back to the earth, that the time for his death has not yet come. At this point he resists, for by now he is taken up with his experiences in the afterlife and does not want to return. He is overwhelmed by intense feelings of joy, love, and peace. Despite his attitude, though, he somehow reunites with his physical body and lives.

Later he tries to tell others, but he has trouble doing so. In the first place, he can find no human words adequate to describe these unearthly episodes. He also finds that others scoff, so he stops telling other people. Still, the experience affects his life profoundly, especially his views about death and its relationship to life.[124]

Others have built on Moody's original work since its publication in the mid 1970s. Reading through this literature certainly offers a meaningful insight into what the subject of an NDE feels and understands, and also reinforces Moody's view of archetypal elements to an NDE. However, despite only coming to the public's attention in recent decades, the experience is hardly a modern invention. Consider the following passages from Graeco-Egyptian magical papyri, in which the dying subject is attempting to ensure immortality or regeneration. "The secret," as Dan Brown says at the beginning of *The Lost Symbol*, is "how to die", and the following archaic instruction manual offers support for that fact. Within it, the individual is instructed on the use of 'magical words' (another major theme of *The Lost Symbol*) during the dying process, in order to navigate the afterlife:

> *When you have spoken in this wise [magical names], you will hear thunder and rushing of the air-space all around; and you yourself will feel that you are shaken to your depths. Then say again: 'Silence'...; thereupon open your eyes and you will see the gates open and the world of the gods within the gates; and your spirit, gladdened by the sight, will feel itself drawn onwards and upwards. Now remain standing still and draw the divine essence into yourself, regarding it fixedly. And when your soul has come to itself again, then speak: 'Approach Lord!' [magic words]. After these words, the rays will turn towards you; and you, focus your gaze on the center. If you do that, you will see a god, very young, beautifully formed, with flame-like hair, in a white tunic with a red mantle and a fiery wreath.*[125]

This passage obviously follows the archetype of the NDE – the hearing of strange noises, the feeling of the spirit being drawn upwards, and an experience with a divine light or being.

The NDE has other parallels in the ancient mystical literature, and – as above – it is generally in terms of instructing the dying individual on navigation of the realms encountered shortly after death. These books therefore provide some support for Dan Brown's suggestion that ancient people were versed in the mysteries of the mind and the post-death existence of the soul. For example, the *Tibetan Book of the Dead* was used as a preparation for what may be experienced by the individual after death, and indeed it has a number of details in common with the NDE archetype including the vision of the light and the sounds heard shortly after death. The *Egyptian Book of the Dead* also suggests an ordeal after death, and many of its passages make much more sense when one has a grounding in the mystical/shamanistic/magical literature.

Furthermore, Yoga – an ancient Indian technique for achieving altered states of consciousness – is said to awaken in the individual abilities which sound very much like those of the shaman and magician, to the extent of echoing the psi-effects mentioned at the beginning of this chapter. The *Yoga Sutras of Patanjali*, compiled around the 3rd century B.C., speak of such abilities – in fact, the third part of the book is entirely devoted to the various 'powers' that are apparently acquired during the practice of Yoga.[126] These are known as *siddhis* – a Sanscrit word meaning "spiritual powers" – and include such skills as seeing and hearing things at a distance (what we know as remote viewing), and the ability to perceive the future (precognition and presentiment). These are abilities that the scientists at IONS are finding evidence for in the modern day – so we can see that, though he obviously writes fiction and embellishes somewhat, Dan Brown was referencing some very real material when he discussed both the 'Ancient Mysteries' and the modern, cutting-edge consciousness research of the Institute of Noetic Sciences in *The Lost Symbol*.

CHAPTER 8

QUEST FOR THE LOST WORD

Dan Brown certainly packed a lot into the 500-plus pages of *The Lost Symbol*. But perhaps the key element to the story is the search for the 'Lost Word', and – in the final pages – Robert Langdon's discovery as to what that actually means. In the early chapters, Langdon explains to Sato that the Lost Word was "one of Freemasonry's most enduring symbols"...

> ...*a single word, written in an arcane language that man could no longer decipher. The Word, like the Mysteries themselves, promised to unveil its hidden power only to those enlightened enough to decrypt it.* "It is said," *Langdon concluded,* "that if you can possess and understand the Lost Word . . . then the Ancient Mysteries will become clear to you."

Later, when Langdon is incredulous at Peter Solomon's insistence that the 'treasure' buried in Washington, D.C. is the Bible, he is counseled that powerful secrets are hidden within its pages: "a vast collection of untapped wisdom waiting to be unveiled." This seems a quantum leap: the 'Lost Word' has jumped from legendary Masonic treasure, to being hidden Biblical wisdom. What is Dan Brown getting at?

The answer lies in one of Brown's major sources for his previous novel: the 'Gnostic Gospels', a collection of early writings about the teachings of Jesus which are not part of the Biblical canon of mainstream Christianity.

The Divine Within

In *The Da Vinci Code*, Dan Brown used a particular concept found in the the Gnostic Gospels to good effect: the idea that Mary Magdalene was of high standing in the early Church, perhaps even being Jesus' partner. In *The Lost Symbol*, Dan Brown has once again mined a rich vein from the Gnostic Gospels: this time, the belief that we are all divine, and that we can all access that divine aspect. The word 'gnostic' comes from the Greek *gnosis*, meaning "knowledge" – the early 'Christian gnostics' who wrote the Gnostic Gospels believed that salvation lay not in faith and worship of God, but in each person having personal knowledge or experience of the divine aspect of their souls. In short, the Gnostic spirituality was about looking within; the divine aspect was immanent, not transcendent. In the words of Elaine Pagels, an expert on the Gnostic Gospels:

> ...*Orthodox Jews and Christians insist that a chasm separates humanity from its creator: God is wholly other. But some of the gnostics who wrote these gospels contradict this: self-knowledge is knowledge of God; the self and the divine are identical.*

As such, Gnostics did not require the help of a church or religious officialdom for salvation – their religion was more a matter of personal exploration. Obviously, this didn't play too well with those who were doing quite well out of organized religion, and so Gnosticism became a heresy. Very little of the Gnostic writings survived the Catholic Church's purge – so much so that it was mostly through the Church's own tirades against Gnosticism that the various Gnostic teachers and schools were known.[127] Then, in December 1945 an Egyptian peasant stumbled across a number of papyrus books stored within a sealed earthenware jar in a cave near the town of Nag Hammadi. The 'Nag Hammadi library' has revolutionized thinking on the origins of Christianity – the leatherbound books contained various 'alternative gospels' and teachings which differ sharply from the content of the canonical gospels. These 'secret' gospels proclaim Jesus as a Gnostic teacher: "These are the secret words which the living Jesus spoke, and which the twin, Judas Thomas, wrote down," says one. Another phrase in the Gospel of Philip gets to the heart of Gnosticism, describing the initiate as "no longer a Christian, but Christ."[128]

So, for all his talk about the Bible being the 'Lost Word', Dan Brown once again is actually seriously undermining the Church with his latest novel, as he is saying that organized religion has subverted the original meaning of the Bible. The underlying message in *The Lost Symbol* is one of rebirth, transformation, and gnosis: various allusions are scattered throughout the book, including Mal'akh's personal life changes, the "rebirthing" technique of the 'Total Liquid Ventilation' tanks, and even when Langdon emerges from the circulation conveyor in the Adams Building ("Langdon felt like he had just emerged from some kind of subterranean birth canal. *Born again*"). Dan Brown is, in fact, preaching the message of the Gnostics: that we all must pursue a personal path to illumination from within, rather than relying on salvation from the Church:

> *You've put your finger on the precise problem! The moment mankind separated himself from God, the true meaning of the Word was lost. The voices of the ancient masters have now been drowned out, lost in the chaotic din of self-proclaimed practitioners shouting that they alone understand the Word...that the Word is written in their language and none other.*

The Mysteries of Gnosticism

In implying that 'the Word' isn't written in just one language, Dan Brown is referencing the long history of gnostic thinking beyond the traditions of the Gnostic Christian sect. For example, he has Peter Solomon note that the figureheads of a number of mainstream religions have espoused gnostic principles in their teachings:

> *Peter lowered his voice to a whisper. "The Buddha said, 'You are God yourself.' Jesus taught that 'the kingdom of God is within you' and even promised us, 'The works I do, you can do...and greater.' Even the first antipope – Hippolytus of Rome – quoted the same message, first uttered by the gnostic teacher Monoimus: 'Abandon the search for God...instead, take yourself as the starting place.' "*

There is actually some evidence that Gnostic Christianity *was* influenced by Buddhist traditions. British scholar of Buddhism Edward Conze has pointed out that trade routes between the Far East and the Mediterranean opened up at the beginning of the Christian era. Conze notes that "Buddhists were in contact with the Thomas Christians (that is, Christians who knew and used such writings as the Gospel of Thomas) in South India," and Buddhist missionaries were spreading their message in the intellectual milieu of Alexandria in Egypt.[129] But Buddhism would not have been the only influence to Gnostic Christians in Alexandria – the city was a literal melting pot of philosophies and religions which would have had some attraction to Gnostics, including Hermeticism and Neo-Platonism. For instance, it is notable that the Nag Hammadi library contains several hermetic works amongst its texts.

Before this mix occurred though, there were earlier mystery religions which had a definite gnostic edge to them – most notably, the 'Ancient Mysteries' of Greece, a term that features often in *The Lost Symbol*. Taking their name from the *mystai* – the blindfolded participants who were about to undergo an extraordinary experience – the Mysteries were said to awaken within the initiate a new appreciation of both life and death. In the words of Cicero, "not only have we received a way of living with prosperity but also a way of dying with greater hope".

The most well-known of these were the Mysteries of Eleusis. Many citizens of Athens took part in these Mysteries, but we still don't know a lot about them as the secrecy of the rituals was heavily guarded – revealing them to non-initiates was considered a crime punishable by death, and in the words of one modern scholar, they "rank among the best-kept secrets of the ancient world."[130] In both the blindfold and the stringent secrecy we can see antecedents to the hoodwink and blood oaths of Freemasonry, though whether there is any direct influence is debatable.

Kevin Clinton, in his essay "The Mysteries of Demeter and Kore", suggests that the most important benefit of the Mysteria was likely that "the initiate gains a better position in the afterlife than the non-initiate." This advantage may have been through a mimicking of the death experience. Clinton cites a passage from the Greek historian Plutarch, in which it is said that at the point of the death, the soul "suffers something like what those who participate in the great initiations suffer." Interestingly, some of these experiences are distinctly similar to the 'Near Death Experience' discussed in the last chapter. There is a journey through darknesss, followed by an encounter with "an extraordinary light", and "pure regions and meadows" with "majesties of sacred sounds." This all sounds very similar to an exhortation in the Gnostic Gospel of Philip which contrasts strongly with traditional Christianity : "Those who say they will die first and then rise are in error. If they do not first receive the resurrection while they live, when they die they will receive nothing..."

Another Greek Mystery religion which some see as a possible influence on Gnosticism was Orphism:

> *The Orphic cult – said to have been derived from the mythic figure of Orpheus – has a number of interesting parallels with Gnosticism: according to Orphic belief, when Dionysus was torn apart by the Titans, shards of his divine nature fell into all human beings, who had yet to be created. When people did finally appear, they had Dionysus' nature within them, often without their realising it. Only those who joined the Orphic cult could be freed from the prison of their earthly existence.*[131]

In their recent book *The Jesus Mysteries*, Timothy Freke and Peter Gandy go so far as to claim that "the Jesus story was not a biography at all but a consciously crafted vehicle for encoded spiritual teachings created by Jewish Gnostics," and was based on the Mysteries of the ancient gods Osiris and Dionysus.

So where does the true origin of Gnostic philosophy lie? Some researchers have speculated that the Great Pyramid of Egypt (*ca.* 2500 BC) was used for initiations into Gnostic-style Mysteries, during which the aspirant would undergo an Out of Body Experience (OBE) and be "born again" upon his return to the material realms.¹³² This idea may have its origin in the thirteenth book of the *Corpus Hermeticum*, in which Hermes Trismegistus explains to his son that "when a man is born again; it is no longer a body of three dimensions that he perceives but the incorporeal."¹³³

It seems though that Gnosticism, in its raw form, is simply a human urge. Before the Christian Gnostics, and the Hermeticists, Neo-Platonists, Buddhists, Jewish mystics and Egyptian initiates, there were the shamans – who could perhaps be seen as the true masters and original progenitors of the Ancient Mysteries.

Masonic Mystery School

What then do Gnosticism, the Bible, and the Ancient Mysteries have to do with Freemasonry and the Lost Word? Consider this description of the Lost Word by the 19th century Masonic scholar Albert Mackey:

> ...*The WORD therefore, may be conceived to be the symbol of Divine Truth; and all its modifications – the loss, the substitution, and the recovery – are but component parts of the mythical symbol which represents a search after truth. In a general sense, the Word itself being then the symbol of Divine Truth, the narrative of its loss and the search for its recovery becomes a mythical symbol of the decay and loss of the true religion among the ancient nations...and of the attempts of the wise men, the philosophers, and priests, to find and retain it in their secret mysteries and initiations, which have hence been designated as the Spurious Freemasonry of Antiquity.*¹³⁴

Many of the early writers on Freemasonry echoed Mackey's view that the Craft was in fact the continuation of secret ancient traditions – the 'Ancient Mysteries' that we have just discussed – in which an initiation led to a personal epiphany and transformation. They also agree that the metaphor of the Lost Word was central to this quest. For instance, Charles H. Vail wrote in 1909 that the Lost Word was symbolic of "the degradation of the Ancient Mysteries...the Word was no mere name, but a knowledge of occult science which could only be attained by soul development."[135] George Steinmetz, in his book *The Lost Word: Its Hidden Meaning*, names the Ancient Mysteries as the "mutual source" of Rosicrucian and Masonic philosophy:

> *What is that source? It can only be the Ancient Mysteries, the original source of all Occult philosophy extant in the world today...the Ancient Mysteries, in harmony with the doctrine of the three-fold man, had as their objective the bringing of man to an intellectual knowledge of his Spiritual Estate, that having cognizance thereof he might develop the spiritual latent within himself, and eventually regain his original status as a* SPIRITUAL BEING, *conscious of his innate spirituality.*

Steinmetz quotes one anonymous writer describing his initiation with the words "Suddenly, I knew as the gods, more cannot be said." Another claims that "At midnight I saw the Sun shining with a splendid light."

The latter testimony offers an interesting parallel with the Masonic search for Light; the "Luciferian Philosophy" which landed Albert Pike at the center of anti-Masonic controversies. There are other curious similarities. The comment in the Gnostic Gospel of Philip, mentioned above – stating that you must be resurrected in life – seems a precursor to the ritual of the Third Degree in Freemasonry, where the Master Mason is 'raised' from his grave during an elaborate initiation ceremony. So does Masonry preserve the Gnostic teachings of the Ancient Mysteries?

Modern Masonic scholars would say no. Extensive research has failed to show any unbroken direct lineage between Freemasonry and earlier mystery teachings and secret societies. Instead, it is assumed that Freemasonry arose from 'Operative Masonry' (groups of actual working stonemasons) and then it evolved with the addition of various "suppositions about Masonry's own past and mankind's spiritual roots."[136]

Albert Pike

Nevertheless, there are hints of influence. Robert Cooper – who has debunked a number of the 'alternative histories' of Masonry – suggests that some aspects of Hermeticism may have found their way into the Craft at the turn of the 17th century via the 'Father of Scottish Freemasonry', William Schaw.[137] And Jay Kinney, in his recent book *The Masonic Myth*, ponders whether Masonic rituals involving the Lost Word originated in the Jewish mystical (and Gnostic-themed) system of Kabbalah. "[I]t seems likely," says Kinney, "that someone conversant with Kabbalistic concepts and symbolism contributed to the evolution of the ritual."

Kinney's view finds support from Henrik Bogdan, a respected scholar of esotericism:

> *[T]he search for a lost word offers an intriguing parallel with zoharic speculations concerning the loss of the proper way to pronounce the name of the Lord, the Tetragrammaton (YHVH). According to kabbalistic tradition, the proper mode of vocalization, or of pronouncing the Divine Name was a guarded secret that was reserved for the Holy of Holies within the temple of Jerusalem.*

> *The second siege of Jerusalem by Nebuchadnezzar in 586 BC that resulted in the destruction of Solomon's temple and the beginning of the so-called Babylonian Captivity of the Jews that was to last until 538 BC, had the consequence that the High Priest no longer had the opportunity to pronounce the name of God. This subsequently led to the tragic consequence that the true way of pronouncing the holy name passed into oblivion. Thus, we find in the zoharic tradition a search for the lost name, or rather the true way of pronouncing a known name.*

> *… At the core of the Jewish Kabbalah lies the fundamental aim of the individual experience of the Godhead, or a Unio Mystica. It is this fundamental aim that links the two traditions together in a functional manner. Both traditions center on a direct identification with, or experience of the Godhead… the aim of the Master degree initiation…aimed at the same goal found in kabbalah, that is, a Unio Mystica.*[138]

As we saw in the early chapters of this book, a number of these Gnostic-styled philosophical systems (Kabbalah, Hermeticism etc.) made their way into Western culture at the beginning of the Renaissance, with the likes of Marsilio Ficino and Giovanni Pico della Mirandola. Indeed, as one source puts it, "Ficino was voyaging through the straits of unorthodoxy out into the open seas of the ancient Gnostic heresies."[139]

So while there may not be a direct lineage to the Ancient Mysteries, it is certainly likely that Ficino and other scholars reintroduced Gnostic elements back into Western civilization which became an 'underground stream' – a syncretic esoteric tradition largely hidden from the view of the profane. Drawing on various influences – from the Ancient Mysteries and Hermeticism through to Islamic Sufism and Jewish Kabbalah – this tradition became known under the moniker of 'Rosicrucianism', before emerging (almost) fully with the official uniting of the lodges in England in 1717. Its goal was personal gnosis, the recovery of the Lost Word – "a return to the primitive and primordial state of man characterized by union with God" through the process of initiation and transformation.[140] No doubt many Freemasons would argue against this, and as the years pass it seems that the Craft seems more and more keen to distance itself from esoteric associations. Earlier Masonic writers had no such problem, disputing the more mundane historical theory of an evolution from organized stonemasonry:

> *Are we to believe that these craftsmen of the medieval guilds, most of whom were actually illiterate, conceived an entire philosophy such as Freemasonry, and then, with consummate cunning, concealed it beneath a complicated system of symbolism and allegory?*[141]

Manly Hall argued that "nearly every great historian of Freemasonry" – including Albert Pike, George Oliver and Albert Mackey – had all "admitted the possibility of the modern society being connected, indirectly at least, with the ancient Mysteries." Meanwhile the French intellectual René Guénon claimed outright that "the masonic institution, through its degrees, contains a powerful esotericism and a 'spiritual influence' leading, as at Eleusis, from the 'Lesser Mysteries' to the 'Greater Mysteries', and opening the path to a unitive vision and to liberation of the soul."[142]

In truth though, we will probably never know the exact origins of Freemasonry. One of the dangers of secret traditions is that, by definition, any 'history' is likely to be deficient or even just plain wrong. And it is in mystical traditions that secrecy is used most extensively. The Ancient Mysteries of the Mediterranean, the Tantric secrets of Hinduism and Buddhism, the mysticism of the Sufis in Islam, the doctrines of the Kabbalists – all are obscured from non-initiates by strict secrecy and the language of symbolism.[143]

What cannot be argued however is that Freemasonry at the very least mimics a Gnostic-style initiatory system akin to the Ancient Mysteries. One of the Brotherhood's most celebrated mystical writers, Walter Wilmhurst, defines the aim of this initiation with symbolism that would please Dan Brown:

> *There remains a way of regaining consciousness of that higher world and life. It is by bringing into function a now dormant and submerged faculty resident at the depth and centre of his being. That dormant faculty is the Vital and Immortal Principle which exists as the central point of the circle of his individuality.*

In writing *The Lost Symbol*, Dan Brown could have had Robert Langdon searching for all manner of material treasures associated with Freemasonry: the body of Jesus, the Ark of the Covenant, the Elixir of Life. It is a credit to him that instead he focused on the 'spiritual treasure' of the Craft. One of Brown's primary sources, the esoteric scholar Manly P. Hall, once wrote that Freemasonry is "a science of the soul." In his earlier Robert Langdon books, Dan Brown explored the tension arising out of the dichotomy of science and religion; in *The Lost Symbol* he may just have resolved it. By putting that 'science of the soul' back into the public consciousness, perhaps it will inspire millions of readers to explore Freemasonry and other offshoots of the Ancient Mysteries, and maybe even to embark on their own process of initiation and pursuit of the divine within.

APPENDIX 1

THE CODES ON THE COVER

In late 2003 it was pointed out to me that the dust cover of Dan Brown's *The Da Vinci Code* contained a number of curious 'anomalies': map co-ordinates in 'mirror writing', bolded letters hiding odd messages, and more. The reason for these strange inclusions became clear when Dan Brown announced in an interview that clues about the sequel to *The Da Vinci Code* were hidden on the cover of the bestselling book. By solving these puzzles and ciphers – and being conversant with many of the topics and resources Brown was likely to use in writing the sequel, I was able to write a complete primer on the as-yet unpublished book in late 2004 (the progenitor of this book you are holding now). In this very early 'guide' to the contents of *The Lost Symbol* – originally titled (and self-published) as *Da Vinci In America* – I gave background information on many of the topics that I surmised would be in the new book: Francis Bacon and the transmission of Rosicrucian philosophies, the history of Freemasonry, how 'the Craft' influenced America's Founding Fathers, and the esoteric landscape of Washington, D.C. (including such exotic locales as the Scottish Rite's "House of the Temple").

When the cover artwork for *The Lost Symbol* was released in July 2009 I received the first confirmation that my research was on the right track. Though only the front cover and spine design was released prior to publication, it was enough to show that various locations in the American capital which I had written about were important to the new book. The cover featured a 'torn parchment' theme similar to the cover of *The Da Vinci Code,* though with Capitol Hill in Washington, D.C. as the focus rather than the Mona Lisa, and the Washington Monument hidden away on the spine. Also prominent was a wax seal emblazoned with a double-headed eagle and the number 33 – a direct confirmation that Freemasonry, in particular Scottish Rite Masonry - would play a major role in the new book.

Not so noticeable on the cover though were the various symbols imprinted upon the parchment, taken from astrology, alchemy and other esoteric fields – and therefore offering the perfect vibe for a Dan Brown book. But on closer inspection, something else became apparent. Once again, Dan Brown had hidden some codes on the cover of his latest novel!

Double-Headed Eagle Emblem of Scottish Rite Freemasonry

Firstly, randomly spread between the front cover and the spine, were letter-number combinations. Above the R of "Brown" we find "B1". On the left, above "a novel", there is another: "C2". And also, on the far right of the cover, "J5". Meanwhile, at the top left of the spine we find "E8", and just above the keyhole at the bottom of the spine is "H5".

Thus, from a scan of the front cover and spine the following codes had been collected: B1, C2, E8, H5, and J5. However, the alphabetical nature of the letter-number combinations – B, C, E, H and J – suggested that at least five more were missing: A#, D#, F#, G# and I# (which would complete the first ten letters of the alphabet, A to J). Without the back cover, the code was unbreakable. Or was it?

A number of (very smart!) people who were working on cracking this code noted that in the previous 'Da Vinci Code Webquest' competition participants were asked to ring the numbers (212) 782-9920 and (212) 782-9932. These numbers seem to be part of a phone number allocation to publisher Random House in New York, whose main number is (212) 782-9000, with the first seven numbers (212-782-9###) being consistent.

The reader has probably already noted that the new cover codes fit this phone number 'template' perfectly. Arranging the five known codes in alphabetical order (ABCDEFGHIJ) gives (#12) #8#-#5#5. Using the known Random House numbers as a base allowed some educated guesses at four of the other letter-number combinations: A2, D7, F2 and G9. This just left I# as the only unknown (212-782-95#5); ten possibilities, easy enough to brute force if someone was willing to call each one.

It turns out a number of people did, but they were met with Random House offices and answering machines – no competition hotline though. This despite confirmation from a newly activated 'Symbol Quest' on Dan Brown's website – in which the participant had to answer 33 consecutive riddles based on various symbols – that, once completed, featured a recording of Dan Brown stating that there were codes on the cover of *The Lost Symbol* which would decode to a telephone number, via which 33 lucky contestants would receive a signed copy of his new book.

As it turns out, the decoding guess was correct – it was just done too quickly! Random House had not 'turned on' the competition phone response at such an early stage. Persistent callers found late on the 14th of September (the day before publication of *The Lost Symbol*) that the competition had gone 'live' on the number (212) 782-9515. A new message was available, from Brown's editor Jason Kaufman, asking contestants to submit an email to a certain address; if they were one of the first 33, they would receive a signed copy of *The Lost Symbol*.

Once released on September 15, the back cover of the book confirmed the decoding: the letter-number combinations A2, D7, F2, G9, and I1 are all found there. It is likely then that anybody that solved the phone number code after buying the book (and seeing the back cover) would have been too late – it's probable that the first 33 emails were received before *The Lost Symbol* even hit bookstore shelves.

But that's not all. There were more codes on the front cover than just these letter-number combinations. On the front cover, just on the inside and outside of the left hand side of the faint circle surrounding the Scottish Rite seal, two sets of numbers can be found:

Outside: 22-65-22-97-27
Inside: 22-23-44-1-133-97-65-44

At first glance, the most notable aspect of this number sequence was the non-random appearance of repeated numbers: 22, 44, 97 and 65. This suggested that the numbers were to be substituted for letters in two words, with 22, 44, 97 and 65 being repeated letters. Further, these repeated numbers in a sequence echoed a code found on the back page of Dan Brown's 1998 book *Digital Fortress:* 128-10-93-85-10-128-98-112-6-6-25-126-39-1-68-78. The solution in that case was that each of the numbers referred to a chapter, and taking the first letter of each of those chapters yielded (after using a further decipher with a 'Caesar Box') the secret message "We are watching you." If this new code used the same deciphering method, it seemed that it could not be solved until the book was published and the first letters of the various chapters known.

Once again, however, brute force deciphering techniques came to the fore. Assuming that the numbers do indeed stand for letters, brute force decoding by substitution analysis can be done by taking into consideration the repeated 'letters', as well as regular English-language use of certain letter combinations and their positions within words. This narrows down the number of possible words that can be represented significantly. Some people are good enough (and have enough spare time!) to do this with paper and pencil, but in the modern age we can be more efficient by utilizing computers to do the job. For example, by converting the number sequence into an equivalent letter sequence – preserving the order and the repeated elements (e.g. ABACD AEFGHCBF) – we can use an online tool such as "Decrypto" (http://www.blisstonia.com/software/WebDecrypto/index.php) to do the work for us. In just 0.022 seconds Decrypto returns only 15 possible word combinations, and for anybody familiar with the content of *The Lost Symbol*, one in particular stands out: "POPES PANTHEON". John Russell Pope is famous for being the architect behind a number of prominent buildings in Washington, D.C., including the National Archives, the Jefferson Memorial, the West Building of the National Gallery of Art, and the Scottish Rite's "House of the Temple". Furthermore, some of these buildings were influenced by the architecture of the Pantheon in Rome, perhaps most prominently the Jefferson Memorial.

Again, this pre-publication solution was confirmed once *The Lost Symbol* was released. Just as surmised, each number pointed to a chapter, from which the first letter was taken and substituted into the sequence. For example, chapter 22 begins with "Pacing", chapter 65 "Once", chapter 97 "Eight", chapter 27 "Systems". Using the first letters of each of these and substituting into the first five numbers of the sequence we get "POPES". Continuing this with the second sequence gives "PANTHEON". A much easier way to decipher the codes obviously, but you still have to admire the ingenuity of the brute force deciphering before publication! Further confirmation that this code points to the Jefferson Memorial comes in the text of *The Lost Symbol*, with Brown twice referencing the monument as being based on the Pantheon.

However, two further codes could only be deciphered once *The Lost Symbol* had been released – simply because they are only on the back cover. Most prominent is the 'Masonic Cipher' (also known as the 'Pigpen Cipher') written just inside the verticals of the decorative frame. To 'read' the symbols in the correct orientation, rotate the back cover 90 degrees clockwise.

Though this is a well-known cipher method and could be decoded without too much help, Dan Brown offers the actual key on page 197 of *The Lost Symbol* (whilst describing it as "almost infantile"). Each symbol is actually the uniquely shaped enclosure of each letter's position in the 'pigpen' grid.

So to start, we have the top-left grid square corresponding to 'A'. The next two are the top right grid-square featuring a dot: 'L'; the first word is "ALL". Continuing on with this deciphering method reveals the statement "ALL GREAT TRUTHS BEGIN AS BLASPHEMIES", which is a quote from the Irish playwright

George Bernard Shaw, and which applies neatly to many of the topics that Dan Brown discusses in his novels.

Lastly, perhaps the most novel cipher technique used by Dan Brown in *The Lost Symbol* is the grid square which is decoded using the number layout in the 'magic square of Jupiter' found in the 1514 engraving *Melencolia I*, by the Renaissance master Albrecht Dürer. As Dan Brown discusses, adding each row, column, and diagonal in this magic square gives a total of 34 (what a shame that wasn't 33!).

Magic square from Dürer's Melencolia I

On the back cover we find there is a grid square containing a number of letters. While again this jumble of letters could be brute-forced if necessary (it baffles Nola Kaye in *The Lost Symbol*, but in reality no C.I.A. analyst would have any trouble with it at all), Dan Brown explains all in the pages of the book. All that is required is to navigate the grid squares in numerical sequence: in Dürer's square, the number '1' is at bottom right, so in the corresponding square in the cover cipher we find a 'Y'. Number '2' is third square in the top row, corresponding to 'O' in cipher square; '3' equals 'U', '4' is "R". Continuing on, the entire message is revealed: "YOUR MIND IS THE KEY", which relates well to the content in *The Lost Symbol* concerning the Ancient Mysteries and Noetic Science.

One final thing worth noting is that Dan Brown has said that there are five hidden messages on the cover. Above I've mentioned four – so what is the final message? It may be the lines mirrored at the top and bottom of the decorative text frame on the back cover, the well-known Hermetic axiom "AS ABOVE SO BELOW", although this hardly seems to be a hidden code. Or does this simply reveal a method for solving a fifth code? Or perhaps a final message is hidden somewhere amongst the various symbols found on the cover? Why not grab your copy and see what you can find. And keep your eye on my Dan Brown-related website The Cryptex (http://www.thecryptex.com) for further updates.

APPENDIX 2

RESOURCES

I have mentioned a number of worthwhile sources in the text of the book, but below I'll provide a comprehensive resource list for those that would like to explore the topics of *The Lost Symbol* in detail. Here are my suggestions, in no particular order (and please note, by listing them I am not vouching for the information in each book or website, just that they will give you insights into various lines of thinking):

Books on Freemasonry and Secret Societies:

- *The Rosicrucian Enlightenment* – Dame Frances Yates
- *Revolutionary Brotherhood* – Steven Bullock
- *Cracking the Freemason's Code* – Robert Cooper
- *The Masonic Myth* – Jay Kinney
- *Solomon's Builders* – Christopher Hodapp
- *Secrets of the Tomb* – Alexandra Robbins
- *Morgan: The Scandal That Shook Freemasonry* – Stephen Dafoe
- *The Mythology of the Secret Societies* – J.M. Roberts
- *A Brief History of Secret Societies* – David V. Barrett

Books on Speculative History:

- *The Secret Architecture of Our Nation's Capital* – David Ovason
- *Talisman* – Graham Hancock and Robert Bauval
- *The Secret Teachings of All Ages* – Manly P. Hall
- *The Temple and the Lodge* – Michael Baigent and Richard Leigh
- *The Secret Destiny of America* – Manly P. Hall
- *The Secret Symbols of the Dollar Bill* – David Ovason
- *The Hiram Key* – Christopher Knight and Robert Lomas
- *The Second Messiah* – Christopher Knight and Robert Lomas
- *The Templar Revelation* – Lynn Picknett and Clive Prince
- *The Stargate Conspiracy* – Lynn Picknett and Clive Prince
- *Shadow of the Sentinel* – Bob Brewer and Warren Getler
- *Born in Blood* – John J. Robinson

Books on Conspiracies:

- *Rule by Secrecy* – Jim Marrs
- *The Brotherhood* – Stephen Knight
- *Inside the Brotherhood* – Martin Short

Books on Noetic Science:

- *Entangled Minds* – Dean Radin
- *The Conscious Universe* – Dean Radin
- *The Field* – Lynne McTaggart
- *The End of Materialism* – Charles Tart
- *Global Shift* – Edmund J. Bourne
- *Irreducible Mind* – Edward F. Kelly et al.
- *Reading the Enemy's Mind* – Paul H. Smith
- *The Stargate Chronicles* – Joseph McMoneagle

- *Experiencing the Next World Now* – Michael Grosso
- *DMT: The Spirit Molecule* – Rick Strassman

Books on Other Related Topics:

- *The Codebreakers* – David Kahn
- *The Faiths of the Founding Fathers* – David L. Holmes
- *The Rosslyn Hoax* – Robert Cooper
- *The Zen of Magic Squares, Circles and Stars* – Clifford Pickover
- *Western Esotericism & Rituals of Initiation* – Henrik Bogdan
- *The Gnostics* – Sean Martin

Websites:

Dan Brown's official website, the center of all things Brownian. Resources for each of his books, links to breaking news, and home to the website challenges as well:

- http://www.danbrown.com/

The Web of Hiram website, an invaluable resource constructed by Robert Lomas on the history of Freemasonry. The website includes masses of historical documents concerning Freemasonry:

- http://www.bradford.ac.uk/webofhiram/

Albert Pike's *Morals and Dogma* online. Read Pike's rambling commentary on comparative religion and esoterica in full, rather than the short quotes often used out of context by anti-Masons:

- http://www.freemasons-freemasonry.com/apikefr.html

The website of the Grand Lodge of British Columbia and Yukon. Detailed essays on the history of Freemasonry, as well as sensible research into the various conspiracy theories regarding the Craft. Hours of great reading available:

- http://freemasonry.bcy.ca/info.html

Website of the Supreme Council 33rd Degree, Scottish Rite Freemasonry, Southern Jurisdiction. Has numerous essays on Scottish Rite Masonry, as well as some beautiful photos of the 'House of the Temple' in Washington, D.C.:

- http://www.srmason-sj.org/

Website of the George Washington Masonic National Memorial. This website features the history behind the building, and provides an excellent tour of the Memorial with images of each room within.:

- http://www.gwmemorial.org/

Archive.org is a great place to search for public domain texts on the history of Freemasonry. Just search the 'Texts' section using related terms ('Freemasonry' etc.):

- http://www.archive.org/

The Kryptos homepage of Elonka Dunin. Everything there is to know about the enigmatic sculpture by James Sanborn – except for the final solution. Perhaps one day soon:

- http://elonka.com/kryptos/

The website of the Institute of Noetic Sciences. Information on the cutting-edge research that IONS is doing into consciousness and intention, along with community-based initiatives which you can be a part of:

- http://www.ions.org/

Wikipedia, the free online community encyclopedia. Information and images on nearly all of the strange topics discussed in this book. All you have to do is search for them:

- http://www.wikipedia.org/

Google's new map feature, which allows you to zoom right in on Washington, D.C. addresses – both in map form and via detailed satellite imagery. A great resource for surveying the design and monuments of the capital. You want detail? You can even see the step-pyramid which surmounts the Scottish Rite "House of the Temple"!:

- http://maps.google.com/

And don't forget to keep an eye on my very own website, The Cryptex, which features news updates and more information about Dan Brown and his books. Any new information uncovered after publication of this Guide will be posted to The Cryptex:

- http://www.thecryptex.com/

APPENDIX 3

A VIEW OF THE CAPITAL

Readers not familiar with the layout of Washington, D.C. may have difficulty in visualizing some of the imagery discussed in this book. This appendix is thus aimed at allowing readers to better understand the relationships between various monuments and landmarks in the capital, through the presentation of a series of maps and views of the city.

Many of these images are historical, showing the gradual evolution of the layout and landmarks of Washington, D.C. Each one is presented as large as possible, and all are accompanied by a few comments to help the reader get their bearings. These maps should allow for a far better understanding of where Robert Langdon is at any one time during *The Lost Symbol*.

Please note that while the included maps are drawn to scale, some of the views do take some artistic licence and should not be trusted as exact representations. They do, however, allow a far better understanding of the city and so are presented here for the reader's benefit.

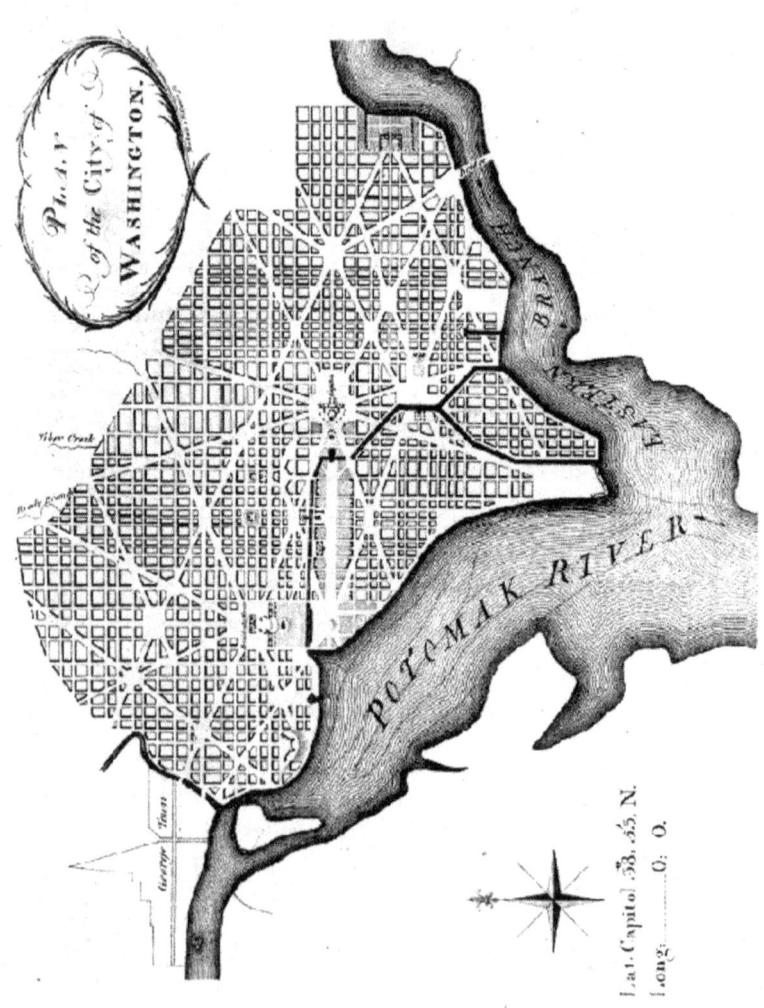

Original Map of Pierre l'Enfant, 1792

This map shows the original plan by Pierre l'Enfant, before any modifications took place. Turn the book ninety degrees clockwise to view north at the top of the page. Note that a lot of the modern layout of the capital can be seen even with this initial design, including the planned locations of the White House, Capitol and the Washington Monument. Similarly, the 'Masonic Compass' design using the Capitol as its mid-point is part of this design. However, numerous other aspects of the street layout were never implemented.

By tracing a line from the planned position of the Washington Monument, to the left (therefore north) through the White House, one can trace out the proposed 'Washington Meridian' mentioned in this book. The Scottish Rite 'House of the Temple' on 16th Street is found on this line, further to the north of the White House.

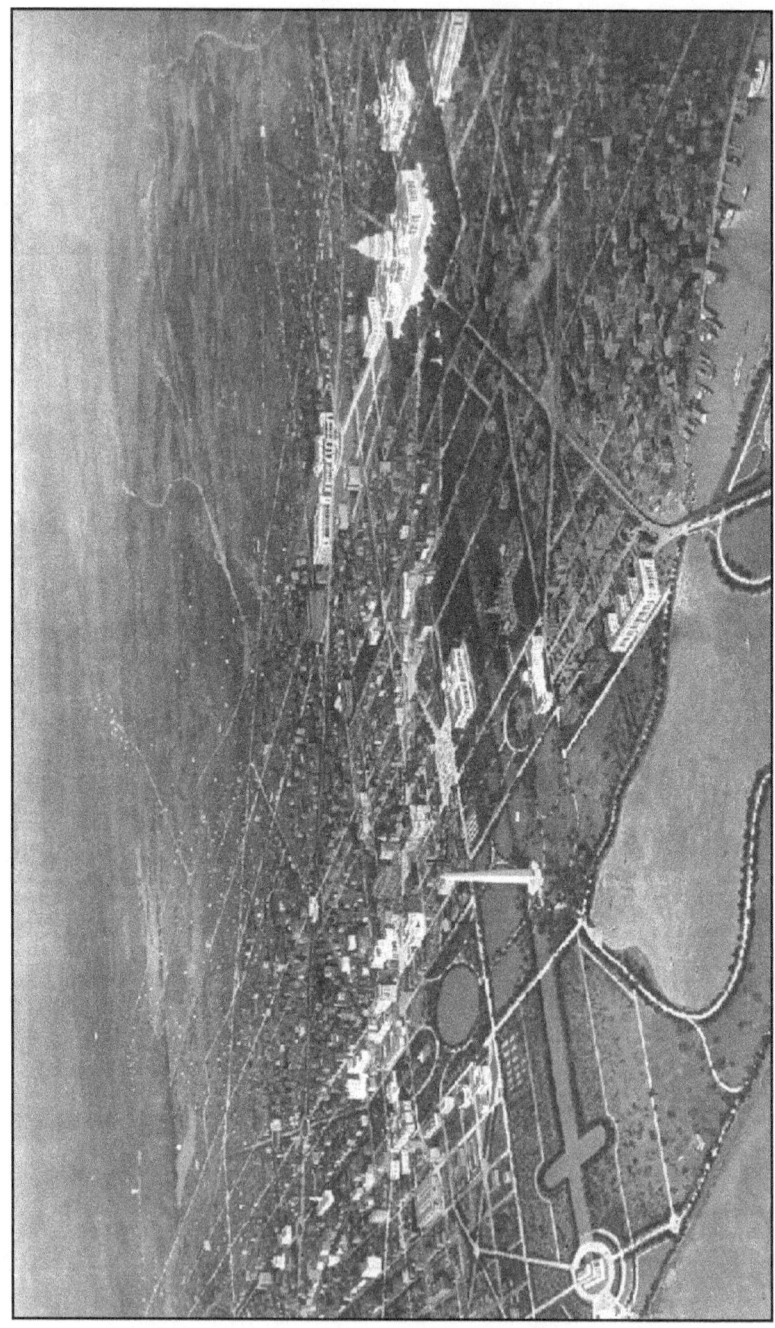

Birds-Eye View Looking North-East

This birds-eye view from almost above the site of the Pentagon building is dated 1916, and shows the limited development of the city, even at the start of the 20th century. The impressive site of the Capitol Building, on Jenkins Hill, is evident in this image. Neither the Jefferson Memorial nor the Pentagon were constructed at the time this image was commissioned – in fact, it would be another two decades before construction of the Jefferson Memorial was undertaken.

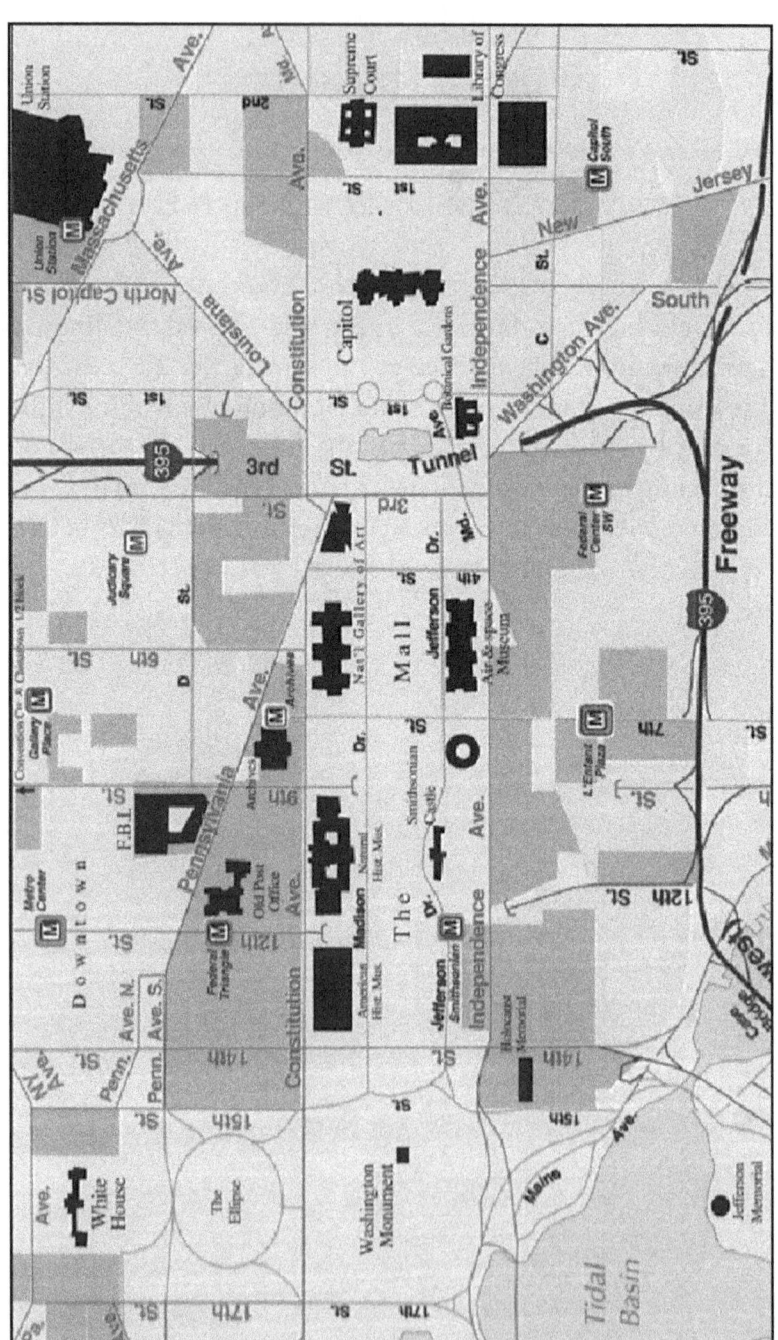

Current Street Map

This simple map shows all the main features of the mall area in Washington, D.C. (once again, rotate clockwise to view north at the top of the page). A lot of the action in *The Lost Symbol* takes place in this area: Langdon moves from the Capitol (east end of the image) to the nearby Library of Congress, and soon after Sato takes Warren Bellamy to the Botanical Gardens, just to the south-west of the Capitol.

The offset of the Washington Monument (western end of the image) from the 'meridian' running through the White House and Jefferson Memorial is quite evident. Just beneath the Federal Triangle can be found the National Gallery of Art as well as the Air and Space Museum (just to the west of the Capitol). Closer to the Washington Monument are the main Smithsonian building ('The Castle'), the American History Museum and the Natural History Museum. The National Archives borders Pennsylvania Avenue. Franklin Square, used as a decoy in Brown's novel, is not visible on this map, but lies just to the west of the White House.

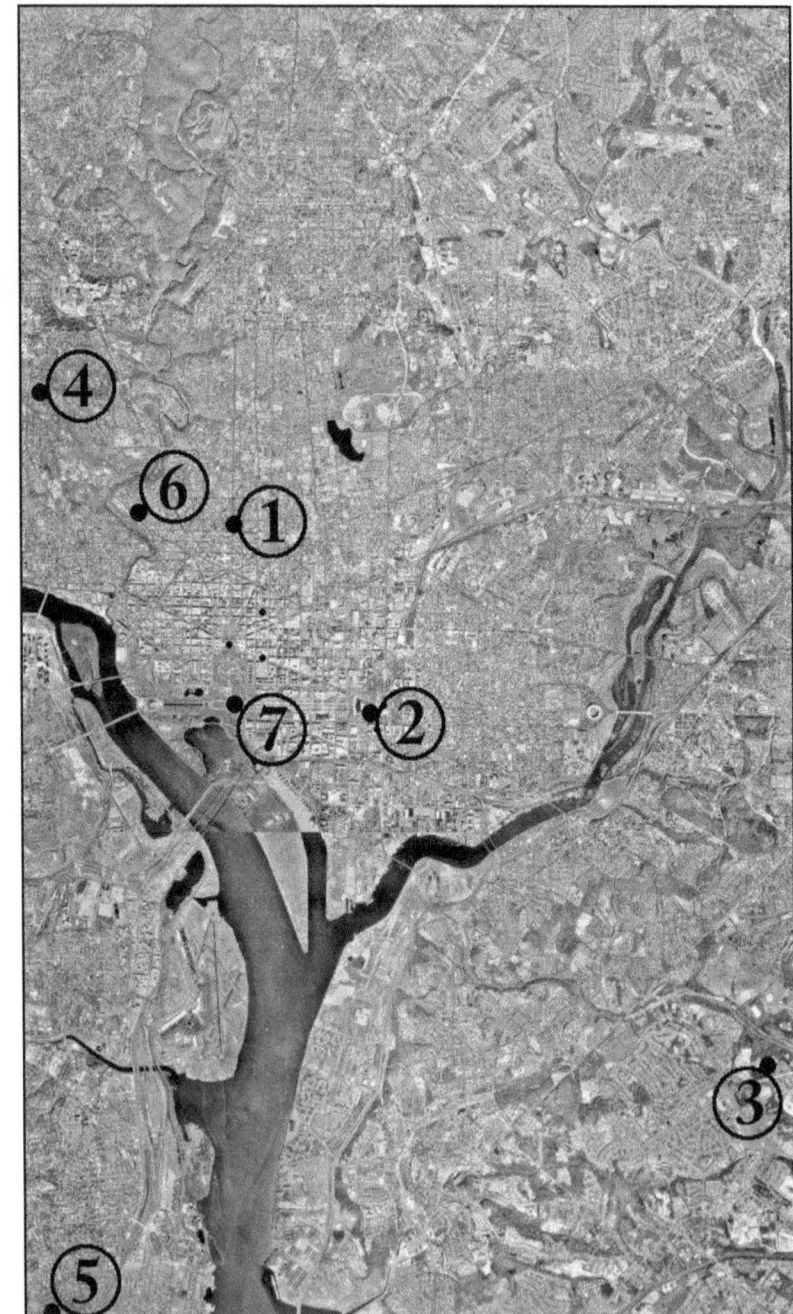

Locations in The Lost Symbol

No need to rotate this map: north is to the top of the page. This image of Washington, D.C. (courtesy of the U.S.G.S.) shows all the main locations in *The Lost Symbol:*

1. The Scottish Rite House of the Temple.
2. The Capitol and nearby Library of Congress/Botanical Gardens.
3. The Smithsonian Museum Support Center.
4. Washington National Cathedral.
5. The George Washington National Masonic Memorial.
6. Kalorama Heights.
7. The Washington Monument.

The three small dots between the House of the Temple (#1) and the Washington Monument (#7) are the White House, Franklin Square, and Freedom Plaza. The headquarters of the Central Intelligence Agency at Langley, Virginia (where Kryptos is located) is not near enough to show on this map – it would be on another another page to the top left.

ENDNOTES

[1] *The Decipherment of Linear B*, John Chadwick, cited in *The Code Book*, Simon Singh

[2] http://www.facebook.com/danbrown / http://www.twitter.com/lostsymbolbook

[3] http://www.danbrown.com/novels/davinci_code/faqs.html

[4] *Western Esotericism and Rituals of Initiation*, Henrik Bogdan

[5] Ibid.

[6] *The Rosicrucian Enlightenment*, Frances A. Yates

[7] "The Rosicrucian Dream", Christopher McIntosh, in *The Inner West*, ed. Jay Kinney

[8] *The Rosicrucian Enlightenment*, Frances A. Yates

[9] Ibid.

[10] Ibid.

[11] *The Way of Light*, John Amos Comenius, trans. E.T. Campagnac

[12] *The Rosicrucian Enlightenment*, Frances A. Yates

[13] King James Bible, I Kings V: 3-5

[14] King James Bible, I Kings VII: 13-21

[15] *The Temple and the Lodge,* Michael Baigent and Richard Leigh

[16] *The Masonic Myth*, Jay Kinney

[17] Ibid.

[18] Cited in "The Hidden Sages and the Knights Templar", Robert Richardson,

in *The Inner West*, ed. Jay Kinney
[19] 'Oration', Andrew Michael Ramsay
[20] Ibid.
[21] Ibid.
[22] *Digging Up Jerusalem*, K.M.Kenyon, cited in *The Second Messiah*, Robert Lomas and Christopher Knight
[23] *Holy Blood, Holy Grail*, Michael Baigent, Richard Leigh, Henry Lincoln
[24] Ibid.
[25] "The Knights Templar in Scotland", R. Aitken, cited in *The Temple and the Lodge*, Michael Baigent and Richard Leigh
[26] *The Second Messiah*, Robert Lomas and Christopher Knight
[27] *The Hiram Key*, Robert Lomas and Christopher Knight
[28] *The Second Messiah*, Robert Lomas and Christopher Knight
[29] *An Encyclopedia of Occultism*, Lewis Spence, cited in *The Templar Revelation*, Lynn Picknett and Clive Prince
[30] *The Temple and the Lodge*, Michael Baigent and Richard Leigh
[31] *Book of Constitutions*, Rev. James Anderson
[32] *Early Masonic Pamphlets*, Knoop, Jones and Hamer, cited in *The Rosicrucian Enlightenment*, Frances A. Yates
[33] "Historico-Critical Inquiry into the Origins of the Rosicrucians and the Freemasons", Thomas de Quincey, cited in *The Rosicrucian Enlightenment*, Frances A. Yates
[34] *The Rosicrucian Enlightenment*, Frances A. Yates
[35] *The Secret Lore of Egypt: Its Impact on the West*, Erik Hornung, trans. David Lorton
[36] *The Secret Symbols of the Dollar Bill*, David Ovason
[37] *The Temple and the Lodge*, Michael Baigent and Richard Leigh
[38] *The Secret Destiny of America*, Manly P. Hall
[39] *The Temple and the Lodge*, Michael Baigent and Richard Leigh
[40] *The Faiths of the Founding Fathers*, David L. Holmes
[41] *The Temple and the Lodge*, Michael Baigent and Richard Leigh
[42] Ibid.
[43] *The Faiths of the Founding Fathers*, David L. Holmes

44 *Talisman*, Robert Bauval and Graham Hancock
45 Wikipedia, http://en.wikipedia.org/wiki/Thomas_Jefferson
46 http://freemasonry.bcy.ca/anti-masonry/jefferson.html
47 Wikipedia, http://en.wikipedia.org/wiki/Thomas_Paine
48 Ibid.
49 *Age of Reason*, Thomas Paine
50 "The Origins of Freemasonry", Thomas Paine
51 Ibid.
52 *Talisman*, Robert Bauval and Graham Hancock
53 "The Origins of Freemasonry", Thomas Paine
54 *The Diary and Sundry Observations*, ed. Dagobert D. Runes
55 *Talisman*, Robert Bauval and Graham Hancock
56 Ibid.
57 Wikipedia, http://en.wikipedia.org/wiki/Haym_Solomon
58 *The Secret Destiny of America*, Manly P. Hall
59 Ibid.
60 Ibid.
61 Cited in *The Temple and the Lodge*, Michael Baigent and Richard Leigh
62 *The Secret Architecture of Our Nation's Capital*, David Ovason
63 http://freemasonry.bcy.ca/anti-masonry/washington_dc/ovason.html
64 *Talisman*, Robert Bauval and Graham Hancock
65 *The Secret Architecture of Our Nation's Capital*, David Ovason
66 *Talisman*, Robert Bauval and Graham Hancock
67 Ibid.
68 http://www.nps.gov/wamo/history/chap2.htm
69 http://www.nps.gov/wamo/history/chap1.htm
70 *Talisman*, Robert Bauval and Graham Hancock
71 *The Secret Architecture of Our Nation's Capital*, David Ovason
72 http://scottishrite.org/visitors/main.html
73 *Shadow of the Sentinel*, Bob Brewer and Warren Getler
74 http://www.fiu.edu/~mizrachs/poseur3.html
75 http://www.cr.nps.gov/nr/travel/wash/dc48.htm

[76] *Talisman*, Robert Bauval and Graham Hancock
[77] *The Great Seal of the United States*, US Department of State
[78] Ibid.
[79] Ibid.
[80] *The Secret Teachings of All Ages*, Manly P. Hall
[81] *The Secret Symbols of the Dollar Bill*, David Ovason
[82] Ibid.
[83] Cited in *America's Secret Destiny*, Robert Hieronimus,
[84] *The Secret Symbols of the Dollar Bill*, David Ovason
[85] *The Secret Architecture of Our Nation's Capital*, David Ovason
[86] *Early Masonic Pamphlets*, ed. D. Knoop, G.P. Jones and D. Hamer
[87] *Talisman*, Robert Bauval and Graham Hancock
[88] "Two Sides But Only One Die: The Great Seal of the United States", M. L. Lien, cited in *Talisman*, Robert Bauval and Graham Hancock
[89] *Occult America*, Mitch Horowitz
[90] *Talisman*, Robert Bauval and Graham Hancock
[91] *Occult America*, Mitch Horowitz
[92] Ibid.
[93] Edgar Cayce, reading 1152-11, cited in *Secret Chamber*, Robert Bauval
[94] "Changing Images of Man", Willis W. Harman, cited in *The Stargate Conspiracy*, Lynn Picknett and Clive Prince
[95] Cited in *Holy Blood, Holy Grail*, Michael Baigent, Richard Leigh and Henry Lincoln
[96] http://www.msnbc.msn.com/id/4179618/
[97] http://msnbc.msn.com/id/3080246/
[98] *Secrets of the Tomb*, Alexandra Robbins
[99] Ron Rosenbaum, cited in *Secrets of the Tomb*, Alexandra Robbins
[100] http://freemasonry.bcy.ca/anti-masonry/anti-masonry05.html
[101] Wikipedia, http://en.wikipedia.org/wiki/Joseph_Smith
[102] *The Da Vinci Code*, Dan Brown
[103] *The Secret Teachings of All Ages*, Manly P. Hall
[104] Ibid.
[105] Ibid.
[106] Ibid.

107 http://www.fbrt.org.uk/pages/essays/essay-ciphers.html
108 *Modern Magick*, Donald Michael Kraig
109 Ibid.
110 Ibid.
111 http://www.monticello.org/reports/interests/wheel_cipher.html
112 "An Assessment of the Evidence for Psychic Functioning", Jessica Utts
113 *The Conscious Universe*, Dean Radin
114 "A Decade of Remote-Viewing Research", Russell Targ
115 "Consciousness and Anomalous Physical Phenomena", Robert Jahn and Brenda Dunne
116 *The Conscious Universe*, Dean Radin
117 Ibid.
118 http://www.swedenborgdigitallibrary.org/ES/epic31.htm
119 *Encyclopedia Brittanica Dictionary*
120 *Shamanism: Archaic Techniques of Ecstasy*, Mircea Eliade
121 *Don Juan, Mescalito and Modern Magic*, Nevill Drury
122 *Metamorphoses*, Lucius Apulieus
123 *Hallucinogens and Shamanism*, ed. Michael J. Harner
124 *Life After Life*, Raymond Moody
125 *Ritual Magic*, E.M. Butler
126 "Psychical Study in India – Past and Present", B.K. Kanthamani, in *A Century of Psychical Research*
127 *The Gnostics*, Sean Martin
128 Ibid.
129 *The Gnostic Gospels*, Elaine Pagels
130 "The Mysteries of Demeter and Kore", Kevin Clinton, in *A Companion to Greek Religion*
131 *The Gnostics*, Sean Martin
132 "The Hidden Sages and the Knights Templar", Robert Richardson, in *The Inner West*
133 *The Gnostics*, Sean Martin
134 *Encyclopedia of Freemasonry*, Albert Mackey
135 *Ancient Mysteries and Modern Masonry*, C.H. Vail

[136] *The Masonic Myth,* Jay Kinney
[137] *Cracking the Freemason's Code,* Robert Cooper
[138] *Western Esotericism and Rituals of Initiation,* Henrik Bogdan
[139] *Dictionary of Gnosis and Western Esotericism,* ed. Wouter J. Hanegraaf
[140] *Western Esotericism and Rituals of Initiation,* Henrik Bogdan
[141] *The Lost Word: Its Hidden Meaning,* George Steinmetz
[142] *Dictionary of Gnosis and Western Esotericism,* ed. Wouter J. Hanegraaf
[143] *Western Esotericism and Rituals of Initiation,* Henrik Bogdan

www.ingramcontent.com/pod-product-compliance
Lightning Source LLC
Chambersburg PA
CBHW051753040426
42446CB00007B/344